WRESTLING WITH GOD:

Evangelicals and the Holy Spirit

Dr. Thomas Reedy

ROAR
PUBLICATIONS

Roar Publications
Kansas City, Missouri

www.roarpublications.com

©2014 Thomas W. Reedy

ISBN - 9781499223347

Table of Contents

Table of Contents

Foreward

Dr. Tom Reedy and I have a spiritual father and son relationship much akin to that of the Apostle Paul and Timothy. He and his wife Kathy are close and dear to my wife Bev and me. I have chosen to honor Tom with this short forward to his new book *Wrestling with God: Evangelicals and the Holy Spirit.*

Tom and I first met in 1988 while he was serving as pastor of Palmcrest Baptist Church in Corpus Christi, TX. We have over the years spoken in his church in Corpus Christi and other places. We walked through and still walk through the results of a horseback riding accident of Kathy and one of their children. Kathy was very seriously injured and still wrestles with the physical results. Both Tom and Kathy are most dear to us. The members of our church, Fullness in Christ Church in Fort Worth, TX have gladly, and with excitement, received every visit Tom has made to our church.

In pursuit of the Holy Spirit, the author has been criticized, challenged and rejected on several fronts. This reaction of the public and the church to Tom made him strong and patient, encouraging him to pursue additional study of the Holy Spirit and the supernatural life. He has grown strong and resolute. That has resulted in him taking on the role of a shepherding pioneer and father in the spirit-filled life movement, the Third Wave movement and in helping the body of Christ explore the delicacies and solutions the Holy Spirit brings to individuals and churches.

This book not only begs a conversation, it gives courage to readers to step out of their comfort zone and have an informed debate first with themselves and then with truth seekers, anointed believers and leaders. Tom illustrates lucidly his paradigm shift by naming evangelical leaders who pointed the way for his own personal journey into "fullness."

As readers, we are encouraged to skip around among the chapters in the order God gives us. I chose Chapter Five: The Missing Dimension of Sanctification/Spiritual Formation. That chapter stirred my memory and heart in analysis of my personal journey into the fullness of the Holy Spirit. Individual names are mentioned of some who influenced us during this season of our journey towards wholeness in God.

The author brilliantly uncovers western rationalism that excludes the supernatural and the

Foreward

spirit-filled life. Sid Roth, a converted Jew, has a daily TV show devoted to "The Supernatural." It is natural to be supernatural. His guest list includes prominent and ordinary people who give testimony and illustrations of this reality. The cat is escaping the bag, and believers are experiencing the Holy Spirit in great numbers.

Pastors, bible students and hungry Christians everywhere will enjoy and be enriched by this book. It can easily be chosen by seminaries and bible schools as required reading and made available in their book stores.

This volume is destined to be on the shelf of hungry, thirsty and inquiring Christians, whose inquiring minds are open to the supernatural. It has the potential to be a best seller! It has my vote.

- Ras Robinson 2014

Preface

In 1985 during a James Robison Bible Conference the author experienced, under the ministry of John Wimber, a powerful encounter with the Holy Spirit.[1] This encounter which included

---

1 The author attended a pastor's conference to hear a man named John Wimber. Wimber believed that the power of God was available to believers as it was during the time of Christ's earthly ministry. This included the supernatural miracles of Jesus. I had gone to the meeting as a skeptic, even bringing with me a tape recorder to reflect on what would be said later.

After many accounts of how God used him (Wimber) miraculously, I reached the point of having to deal with some conflicting opinions, i.e., his and my own. I somehow knew that he was sincere, but I found it hard to believe what he was saying. He said, "Those of you who find it hard to believe what I am saying please stand if you want to receive something from God." In an auditorium of about two thousand people I was one of two hundred that stood. He asked the Holy Spirit to come into the meeting, and for the next twenty minutes people wept and cried out loud all over the auditorium. I, myself, for no explicable

i

surges of what felt like electricity running though my arms and hands was accompanied by a new awareness of the presence of God, the ability to hear the voice of God internally in my spirit, and the ministry of healing followed later by the authority to cast out demons. This new found position in Christ came to me at a time when I was hungry for more of God, yet at the same time skeptical about all things associated with Charismatic/Pentecostal experience. As a Southern Baptist pastor who had graduated with a Masters degree and a Doctor of Ministry degree from Southwestern Baptist Theological Seminary, I had been taught to rely solely on the bible and to question all experiences not in tune with the

_____

reason, began to weep. With my rational processes in a state of bombardment, I began to experience for the first time a sense of power (*dunamis*) flowing through me like waves of electricity. The sensation was strongest in my arms and hands. This went on for the entire twenty minutes. Toward the end of the event God brought the scripture to my mind that says, "not with words of human wisdom, but in demonstration of the Spirit and of power" (1 Cor. 2:4). Though shaken, I remember laughing because I realized what Wimber had done. He did not intend to convince the skeptic with a rational argument. He instead practiced what he had preached, and called upon a demonstration of the Spirit's power to back up his argument-testimony.

interpretations I had received from my professors. After eight years in pastoral ministry as a Baptist, I found my entire understanding changed regarding God's view of His Holy Spirit and what it meant to be baptized/filled with the Spirit of God.

In the past while I was involved with Campus Crusade on the campus of Baylor University, I had prayed many times to be filled with the Spirit according to the little blue pamphlet "How to be Filled with the Spirit." Each time I was instructed that after the prayer for infilling was done, I should just simply believe that God had filled me. So I spent a number of years believing that being Spirit-filled was an intellectual, doctrinal position that one simply had to take for granted if one complied with the formula of the scripture as propagated in the pamphlet. Still, nothing changed. This Baptist pastor was still unable to do anything in a supernatural way. I had no supernatural power. It was at the conclusion of finishing my dissertation, which was on the subject of ecclesiology (the study of the church), that I realized that there was a great gap between the expression of the life of the early church and the kind of church life that I was currently experiencing. This was the beginning of a hunger of desiring to know if there was something more to the Christian experience beyond salvation.

Before I made the decision to go and hear John Wimber speak at the James Robison Bible Conference, I had already hit a theological wall having listened to one of Wimber's tapes (provided by an individual who thought I would benefit from the tape spiritually). The crucial snag was the scripture passage that states:

> Philip said, "Lord, show us the Father and that will be enough for us." [9] Jesus answered: "Don't you know me, Philip, even after I have been among you such a long time? Anyone who has seen me has seen the Father. How can you say, `Show us the Father'? [10] Don't you believe that I am in the Father, and that the Father is in me? The words I say to you are not just my own. Rather, it is the Father, living in me, who is doing his work. [11] Believe me when I say that I am in the Father and the Father is in me; or at least *believe on the evidence of the miracles* (my emphasis) themselves. [12] I tell you the truth, anyone who has faith in me will do what I have been doing. He will do even greater things than these, because I am going to the Father. [13] And I will do whatever you ask in my name, so that the Son may bring glory to the Father.

14 You may ask me for anything in my name, and I will do it. "(John 14:8).

John Wimber stated that the greater works that we would be doing meant greater miracles. I had been taught that the "works" was simply preaching the gospel, and the greater works was being able to preach the gospel through the media. My instructors emphasized a rendering of the Greek that emphasizes the notion of "greater in number," but after studying the Greek term, it could also be rendered "greater in kind." Clearly, the context had to do with miracles. Having been taught to believe the Bible, I now found that my experience and the scriptures were not in agreement. I had to either invalidate the scriptures, or I had to admit my experiences to-date were inadequate and below the expectations of Jesus regarding my ministry. I was the "anyone who has faith in me (Jesus)," yet I was not seeing the "greater works." The choice was simple-believe God's word was true or deny it. I could put my faith in my lack of experience (an act of trusting experience in its own right) or seek the kind of experience the scripture spoke of. Even though I was not completely sure what I was missing or how to go about receiving any new experiences from God, I decided to go to the conference to look for answers to my new-found dilemma.

When God encountered me through his Holy Spirit, I not only received power (as Jesus spoke about in Luke 24:48-49 and Acts 1:8), but I also began to hear his voice in a new way. He actually would carry on conversations with me in my head and later I would receive "pictures" (what the bible calls visions- cf. Acts 2:17-21 in a reference to Joel 2:28-32) that would require further conversation with Him in order for me to understand what they meant. I would later understand that these manifestations of the Holy Spirit were what Paul talked about in 1 Corinthians 12:7-11 when he spoke about words of wisdom, words of knowledge, and prophecy. More importantly, for evangelicals, the experience with the Baptism/filling of the Holy Spirit (I use a combination term because evangelicals prefer filling to the term baptism) is a door to supernatural living. For me, the initial filling, called baptism, is in keeping with a subsequent work of the Spirit (which is generally denied by evangelicals) resulted in a deeper walk with Christ, as the fruit of the Holy Spirit (Gal. 5:22) began to be expressed in me and through me in an increased way. I was filled with JOY. My LOVE for Christ at times was overwhelming. In short, everything about God was more real or should I say *more tangible*. God became immanent and not just transcendent. The change in my life was immediately noticeable to my Baptist congregation. The church began to grow. My sermons were more impactful. However, the fear of becoming something other than Baptist was too much for the church and resulted in me becoming a pastor of another Baptist church, which was more open to the Holy Spirit. It was during the five years that I was the pastor of a "Spirit-filled" Baptist church[2] that I began to notice that no matter how much we pursued allowing the Holy Spirit to direct our lives and the life of our congregation, we seemed to hit a kind of ceiling in how much freedom was considered appropriate. Having been associated with Spirit-filled Baptist churches and their pastors, I was perfectly at home with being a Baptist (evangelical) and also being "filled" with the Holy Spirit. However, there seemed to always be a kind of cautious tension, a kind of

---

2   Evangelicals, and Baptists in particular, consider all Christians Spirit-filled because of the initial indwelling of the Holy Spirit at the time of salvation. I have put the term in quotations to indicate that the use of the term as I use it is in dispute and considered by some to be offensive. It is not my intent to say evangelicals do not have the Holy Spirit, but I simply use the term to indicate a certain theological orientation regarding the role of the Holy Spirit in the Life of the church.

wariness towards fully trusting the Holy Spirit, while at the same time enjoying worship, the healings, and the vibrant relationships He encouraged. It was only after the Lord spoke to us about becoming a non-denominational church (stepping away from the denominational tag) that I realized we/I had been held back by a "cultural" understanding of what church life was supposed to be about. This raised a serious question in my mind. Why is it that the "Spirit-filled" evangelical/Baptist churches I had been a part of were mostly "evangelical" with some Holy Spirit on the side? I believe in part the reason for this observation was because there was a commitment to serve as a bridge or accommodate evangelical sensitivities toward the working of the Holy Spirit. Yes, there was a commitment to reformed theology, but the seeming boundaries that enforced a commitment to a traditional evangelical perspective were more cultural than anything else. It was not chiefly a matter of doctrine, because even though I changed my doctrine I felt constrained by certain evangelical boundaries that were clearly part of the culture. In short, I wanted to keep my current associations (with friends and ministry contacts). My advanced ministry training was not as valued among certain Charismatics who saw the intellect has an adversary to the Holy Spirit, and I would have to leave my comfort zone and be willing to accept a new kind of diversity of people I was unfamiliar with. This problem was highlighted to me on several occasions, but I will mention at least one

I asked a fellow Baptist pastor, who also had his doctorate, why Baptist churches had congregational voting, since this process is not reflected in the scripture (a non-biblical practice). He said he knew the practice was not biblical, but he valued his job and would refuse to do anything about it. While I was not suggesting he should cause a firestorm in his church, I wanted to know whether or not being "biblical" was a value of the church we were a part of. I came to realize the "customs" (culture) of the congregation/church played a role in the identity of the people, whether or not it was biblical. Apparently, the doctrine of "the priesthood of the believer" did not only refer to one's relationship with God, without the need of a human mediator (as maintained from the time of the Reformation), but instead appeared to be connected with the American democratic notion of "one man one vote." I am not against consensus. However, when the will of God is determined by 51% of a vote, then God appears to be almost borderline schizophrenic in terms of expressing his will regarding two mutually exclusive options. Furthermore, there are plenty of examples when the minority opinion was right and the majority was wrong, if not oppressive. In contrast, there are evangelical churches that are governed by an elder system that has devolved into a kind of dictatorship; the scripture deals with those kinds of situations. As long as there are people trying to "run" the church, there will be problems in the system. Nonetheless, the elder system is at least "biblical." Thus, I learned that the problem did not have to do with doctrine that is derived from scripture, but a commitment to the "way we do things around here." This is called "orthopraxy" (how things are done in order to be accepted) as opposed to "orthodoxy" (the things you must doctrinally believe to be accepted). Now, I am using these terms in a non-traditional way. "Ortho" implies that which is the norm or correct understanding of something as opposed to heresy, which is a deviance from the norm. The problem is one person's orthodoxy is another person's heresy. To the Catholics, the Protestants were heretics (including the Anabaptists); to the premillennialists, the postmillenialists are heretics; and to the Calvinists, Arminians a heretics. Dr. Bruce Corley, my New Testament professor at Southwestern Baptist Theological Seminary ,called "Dispensationalism"(Hal Lindsey and the *Left Behind* series) a heresy. I agree. Perhaps what we need, however, is a conversation

Preface

(not an inquisition), led by the Holy Spirit, anchored in scripture and involving higher critical thinking skills, not emotional, bias-laden, and defensive posturing.

This book is about provoking that conversation. The use of the word "provoke" is intentional. All good interactive conversations begin when someone is "forced" to examine his or her beliefs. There is the risk that this book will be discarded before it is completely read. However, even if it causes no re-examination of one's belief, this work is still valuable if you want to be able to defend your position. It is helpful to know the arguments that challenge your position, so that you may address them when faced with these issues in the future. As an apologetics teacher at a Christian school, my responsibility is to get my students to think critically about the Christian faith and to defend their position. This will not happen apart from exposing them to alternative views and then having a serious discussion about the Bible and what constitutes a Christian worldview. While theological differences within the orthodox Christian community is not the substance of the course, the process of thinking biblically and theologically using higher critical thinking skills is a part of the course. It is my prayer that this book will begin a process of genuine connection with the Lord Jesus Christ through the

Holy Spirit.

I have tried to construct the order of chapters to best lead you through a specific path of thinking. As a reader it is your prerogative to jump to any chapter you wish to read. However, as a teacher, I may refer back to previous chapters and the answer to questions or even objections may have been dealt with earlier. Additionally, the footnotes, which are sometimes ignored by readers, are very important because I give specific interpretive explanations regarding scripture passages and use them to answer possible objections. In short, it is very helpful to read the footnotes. I use them in order not to break the line of reasoning in the book. Finally, there may be some ideas that are different than what you have believed. I know how that feels. Only the Holy Spirit can convince you of the things I have stated in the book. To that end, it is best to seek His guidance in prayer and not to become defensive about what you are about to read. I trust you have come into possession of this book because you are interested in knowing more about living the Christian life by the Spirit of God. Perhaps you realize there is something more to the Christian life than what you are experiencing, or you feel like the evangelical church needs a new dimension in the Spirit if it is going to be effective in these last days. For those of you who have already experienced the supernatural realm of the Spirit, this book was also birthed out of the need to explain (defend?) a reality than I have known since 1985. At the end of the book, as an encouragement, I have included the testimony/journey of man I have mentored for over eight years. At times this book will be encouraging, at times provoking, but most of all it will be a challenge to lay aside some preconceived notions about the life and ministry of the Holy Spirit in order to come into a more intimate relationship with Him. He is the Spirit of Jesus inside you.

Chapter One: The Influence of Western Rationalism

As American Christians one of the more ~~unfortunate aspects of our culture is the pervading~~ influence of Western Rationalism.[3] This dominate world-view of American and European society removes the supernatural in matters regarding the Christian life. Christians in other parts of the world are more familiar with the everyday aspects of the supernatural in their culture, particularly in countries belonging to the African continent. Such believers are

---

3 Western Rationalism, as a world-view, is the cultural viewpoint that the world and all the phenomena associated with it can be explained through natural (not supra [above] natural) means. This world-view utilizes the powers of the mind to interpret events and the material aspects of the world as a closed system, i.e., being unaffected by anything beyond the natural order. Thus, all that may be learned or experienced can be known through the five senses and the explanation for things that occur in the natural realm may be explained as being caused solely by natural phenomena. For example, sickness is *always* caused by germs etc. and not by demons or other non-natural causes.

aware of both demonic encounters and the presence of religious influence that emphasize the need to deal with supernatural phenomena as a matter of daily existence. The experiences of these believers, as well as non-believers alike, may be dismissed as superstitious, but, increasingly, missionaries and others are validating the presence and activity of the demonic in other countries. The only counter to these demonic spirits is the active ministry of the Holy Spirit in these areas. Missionaries are forced to come to terms with deliverance (casting out of demons) and issues of healing in a culture that recognizes the supernatural and often utilizes witch doctors and shamans as spiritual alternatives. Thus, some of the fastest growing denominations (the Assemblies of God and other Pentecostal/spirit-filled congregations) in these countries are the ones that directly address these spiritual realities as opposed to denying their existence. More importantly, the reality of the supernatural is not something that is only valid in these countries, but is applicable to American society and culture, even if the culture is Western Rationalism. The reason for this is obvious. In matters of the spiritual realm, if there is truth to the notion that demons exist in other countries, then it is also true that demons inhabit western culture as well, even if their presence is denied.

According to the Bible, these evil spirits have not left the world, nor are their presence solely limited to certain sections of the globe. In this regard, the doctrine (scripture) about demons is a matter of "absolute" truth as opposed to "truth" from a relativistic position.[4] Thus, if there are demons in Africa, there are demons in America, as well, even if American Western Rationalism denies the truth/reality of the matter. This alone should be enough to give American Christians pause to be concerned; but in addition to the reality of the demonic in the world today, it should be understood that the culture of the Bible is Middle Eastern and not based on the culture of Western Rationalism. Therefore, many American/Western Christians have a cultural disconnect between the world of the Bible and the world in which they live. American Christians profess to believe the Bible, the same Bible that speaks about the reality of demons in the world, supernatural power for healing, miracles, visions and angelic

---

4 Relativistic truth is the idea that something may be "true" for one person or group of people because they believe it to be true, but at the same time may not be true to others simply because they do not believe it to be true. Under this rubric or way of looking at things, there is no strong definition of truth as being something that is universally applicable to all people.

3

encounters, yet at the same time deny such absolute truth experiences as being part of the world in which they live. Consequently, their mind and experiences, reinforced by unbelief, prevent them from seeking or even acknowledging there may be a supernatural realm that they are called to experience.[5]

I have focused on the presence and reality of demons for a specific reason. While, healing and other matters are also just as supernaturally real, there are those who acknowledge the demonic even if they do not accept the reality of God's Spirit as being at work in the world today. Such an opinion is represented in a theological system of belief known as "dispensationalism."[6] As a result of this system

---

5 The problem with this world-view is that the human mind (reasoning) is placed above the truth of the Bible. The mind, in essence, denies the truth of the Bible, because the individual has not experienced the supernatural because of unbelief. What happens is a vicious cycle of experience and unbelief. Unbelief inhibits the individual from experiencing the supernatural, and the experience of the individual re-enforces the idea that the supernatural is not real because it has not been experienced. Jesus reverses the notion of "seeing is believing" by inverting it. He states "Did I not tell you that you would see God's glory if you believed" (John 11:40).

6 Dispensationalism is the name of a belief system that

of belief, certain believers do not believe that God works supernaturally today, but instead, they are concerned that they may be deceived by false "signs and wonders." However, the fact remains if there is the existence of the false, then there must also exist its counterpart, the true. The church today must come to a place where they see God as involved in the affairs of humanity as the devil, and He does not take a back seat to the devil in matters of supernatural displays of power. A weak and powerless church would be a testimony to the failure of the gospel of the kingdom.

---

maintains that God has dealt with humanity in a number of different ways (dispensations). For our purposes there are some specific tenets of dispensationalism that has made its way into the collective cultural consciousness of the church that has become an obstacle to those who find it difficult to accept the full range of the Holy Spirit's activity today. Such tenets are: 1. Miracles/supernatural events ceased (called Cessationism) at the end of the apostolic age of the first century; 2. The world will become more evil and the church will be under attack and weakened as many are deceived by the devil and find that their love for God begin to grow cold; and 3. There will be signs and wonders performed by the devil and his agents so as to deceive believer's into taking the mark of the beast.

Chapter Two: The Need for Living the Supernatural, Spirit-filled Life

There seems to be an idea that exists in the church that the Spirit-filled life is an option that believers may choose or choose to ignore. This is basically predicated upon the notion that those who emphasize the Holy Spirit do so as some aspect of their own pet doctrine, and those who attempt to explore or experience something from the Holy Spirit somehow abandon their own doctrinal emphasis or even a deny their identity. In short, it could be perceived by those with whom we have a relationship as a kind of betrayal or abandonment of the community and the close relationships in the community. Therefore, a price is paid to stray from the basic beliefs, if not cultural tenants of one's denomination. However, Charismatic believers and Pentecostal believers have not cornered the market on things dealing with the Holy Spirit. Church history is replete with examples of the Holy Spirit moving among denominations, even Methodists and Baptists, during the western expansion of the church in America. [7] John Wimber in his the appendix of his book *Power Evangelism* details the history of the supernatural occurrences in the life of the church through well-known Christian leaders–such as Luther, Wesley and others.

The fact remains that the church needs the supernatural power of the Holy Spirit now as it was in the first century. This is especially true if the days are growing darker (more evil) as the coming of Christ draws near. More importantly, however, and even more basic to Christian living is the admonition that the apostle Paul makes to the church at Ephesus, when he tells the believers there, "Do not get drunk on wine, which leads to debauchery. Instead, be filled with the Spirit" (Ephesians 5:18 NIV). The force of the verb "be filled" is in an imperative present tense continuous action form. In other words Paul is commanding the church to be continuously or constantly filled with the Spirit. A believer is to be filled up with many new fillings following. This command to be filled makes the Spirit-filled life not an option, but a requirement. When commands are

---

7 The Cane Ridge Rival in the 1800s saw tremendous manifestations among Baptists who attended revival meetings (called camp meetings). Baptists shuddered, fell down, staggered from the meetings and even in come instances barked like dogs.

disobeyed it is disobedience or sin. Because Paul was inspired by the Spirit to write these words it is not just Paul's command, but it is God's command as well.

Jesus Christ (Christ is the Greek form of the Hebrew word Messiah, which means "anointed") has as his title the word Christ, which is derived from the Greek word *Charis*. The word *Charis* forms the basis of the concept of "grace" and is part of the term *Charis*matic. In essence, Jesus, the anointed one (Charis-matic one) is the model of ministry for believers of all generations. He is the prototype of what it means to be a human being operating under the grace of God in fellowship with God.

Many believers give up the notion of a supernatural ministry because they believe that Jesus, being the one and only son of God, ministered out of his "Godness."[8] However, this idea is incorrect. Jesus called himself "the Son of Man" for a reason. Jesus came to earth not only to save us, but also to show us the kind of life that God has called us to live. He is our example in life and ministry–both were

---

8 If Jesus ministered supernaturally because he is the only Son of God, i.e., he ministered out of his godness, then that lets believers off the hook. It is asserted that we are not like him; therefore, we cannot minister like him. He is God and we are not.

supernaturally inspired. The key to understanding the ministry of Jesus rests in his relationship with the Father through the anointing he received by the Holy Spirit. After his baptism, the Spirit of God came upon Jesus (a matter he was to refer to later when he read from Isaiah 61:1-21a as recorded in Luke 4:18-19), then sent him into the wilderness to be tested.[9] The test was about whether or not Jesus would rely upon the Father as a perfectly submitted human son or whether he would use his power as God (or his status as God's divine son). Jesus chose to be a perfectly submitted (fully human) son, something that we are asked to do toward God, Jesus and the Holy Spirit. Out of this submission to the Holy Spirit Jesus moved in power. It is a mistake to believe that Jesus ministered out of the privilege of His divinity. That is clearly not the lesson he taught his disciples. Jesus reminded his disciples that he only did what he saw the Father doing and that the words he taught came from the Father himself; they were not his own words. This represents a complete and total reliance on the Father. *The power Jesus had came by way of the Holy Spirit*, who is God and the expression of the will of the Father's heart. A key to this understanding is found in a verse that was been

9 Matthew 4:1-11.

previously mentioned. In John 14: 8 Jesus says:

> Philip said, "Lord, show us the Father and that will be enough for us." 9 Jesus answered: "Don't you know me, Philip, even after I have been among you such a long time? Anyone who has seen me has seen the Father. How can you say, `Show us the Father'? 10 Don't you believe that I am in the Father, and that the Father is in me? *The words I say to you are not just my own. Rather, **it is the Father, living in me**, who is doing his work.* [my emphasis] 11 Believe me when I say that I am in the Father and the Father is in me; or at least *believe on the evidence of the miracles* [*the work of the Father living in Jesus*, my comment] themselves. 12 I tell you the truth, anyone who has faith in me will do what I have been doing. He will do even greater things than these, because I am going to the Father. 13 And I will do whatever you ask in my name, so that the Son may bring glory to the Father. 14 You may ask me for anything in my name, and I will do it.[10]

---

10 The word "works" in the Greek is a general word for anything a person might do. It must be interpreted

My point here is pretty simple. Jesus set a pattern for ministry from his own life, and it was carried on through the ministry of the apostles and on through various segments of the church past the first century. There is no other pattern of ministry that is given to believers except that which he gave, and he encouraged the disciples to pass this style

---

through the context in which the word appears. In this case, the subject was about believing on the miracles that Jesus performed that proved he and the father were one. Thus, when we do the same or greater works that Jesus mentions, then we also demonstrate that our ministry, like his, is from God. A key to understanding **what Jesus did** may be found in at least two passages: 1. (Acts 10:38) ". . . how God anointed Jesus of Nazareth with the Holy Spirit and power , and how he went around **doing** good and healing all who were under the power of the devil, because God was with him." and 2. (John 3:1-2) where Nicodemis tells Jesus that he is from God because no one could **do** what he did if he were not from God. Clearly, Jesus performed miracles and they were no small part of his ministry. He did not just preach and teach, but he demonstrated the power of the kingdom wherever he went. The miracles were not just to validate his ministry, but were also to set an example of what ministry would be all about. His disciples understood this and performed supernatural feats in their ministry. This supernatural dimension of ministry indeed carried past the first century into the ministry of those who would come later.

of ministry on to other believers when he states, "Therefore go and make disciples of all nations, baptizing them in the name of the Father and the Son and the Holy Spirit, and *teaching them to obey everything I have commanded you* [my emphasis]. And surely I am with you always, to he very end of the age" (Matthew 28:19-20). Evangelicals have a good track record in winning the lost and baptizing them, but what about teaching these new converts to do everything Jesus told the disciples to do (teaching them to obey everything I have commanded you). What did Jesus command his disciples to do? In Luke 9:1-9, the disciples are given power to drive out demons and cure diseases. They are told "to preach the Kingdom of God and to heal the sick." Their success in this mandate caused the people to believe "that Elijah had appeared." Later, seventy-two others [that is more that just the twelve disciples] reported back to Jesus telling him "that even demons submit to us in your name" (Luke 10:17). It is recorded that in response to this declaration Jesus was filled with joy (literally: danced or twirled with joy). Even if a desire to live a supernatural life of ministry in the Holy Spirit is not something that one could easily embrace at this juncture of one's walk that does not mean that the normal Christian life can be lived apart from the Holy Spirit's influence.

In conclusion, being filled with the Spirit, "anointed," or whatever we chose to call this relationship with the Holy Spirit, is absolutely essential for experiencing the kind of relationship that Jesus died on the cross to give us. Jesus did not simply die on the cross in order to give us heaven or eternal life, even though he states that he was sent into the world to save the world or save the lost (John 3:17). In other equally important scriptures about the mission of Jesus, we find that He came in order to destroy the works of the devil (by the cross and the casting out of demons)–"For this purpose was the Son of God manifest: to destroy the works of the evil one" (1 John 3:8) and that he came in order that we should be able to live the empowered Spirit-filled life. Jesus states:

> **I have come to bring fire on the earth**, and how I wish it were already kindled! [50] *But I have a baptism to undergo*, and how distressed I am until it is completed! [51] Do you think I came to bring peace on earth? No, I tell you, but division. [52] From now on there will be five in one family divided against each other, three against two and two against three. [53] They will be divided, father against son and son against father, mother against

> daughter and daughter against mother, mother-in-law against daughter-in-law and daughter-in-law against mother-in-law (Luke 12:48 49).

Jesus is telling his disciples that he has come to bring fire on the earth, the very fire that John the Baptist spoke of when he said, ""I baptize you with water for repentance. But after me will come one who is more powerful than I, whose sandals I am not fit to carry. **He will baptize you with the Holy Spirit and with fire** [my emphasis]. 12 His winnowing fork is in his hand, and he will clear his threshing floor, gathering his wheat into the barn and burning up the chaff with unquenchable fire "(Matt 3:11). In this passage there is also a connection with the "winnowing" or dividing process that is found in Luke 12:51-53. Jesus died on the cross not to give us only heaven, but an eternal life that is supernaturally lived out on earth. The fire that came to earth is the power of the Holy Spirit that Jesus promised in Acts 1:8 when he says, "But you will receive power when the Holy Spirit comes on you; and you will be my witnesses in Jerusalem, and in all Judea and Samaria, and to the ends of the earth." This power is supernaturally evidenced in Acts 2:1-4 which states:

When the day of Pentecost came, they were all together in one place. ²Suddenly a sound like the blowing of a violent wind came from heaven and filled the whole house where they were sitting. ³They saw what seemed to be **tongues of fire that separated and came to rest on each of them [my emphasis].**⁴ All of them were filled with the Holy Spirit and began to speak in other tongues as the Spirit enabled them.

Faithfulness to the cross means we must honor Jesus for all that he purchased for us on the cross. The cross is not the stopping place in the gospel, only the beginning place. Jesus died on the cross, was buried, resurrected and ascended on high in order for the Holy Spirit to come and live in the hearts of believers and to empower them to live a supernatural life and do His works. In fact, Jesus told his disciples that it was important for him to go away in order that the Holy Spirit (the comforter) would come.[11]

---

11 "It is for your good that I am going away. Unless I go away the comforter will not come to you" (John 16:7). This going away that Jesus refers to is his death on the cross (his baptism that he must undergo). He has to die on the cross (complete his mission of salvation) in order for the

15

The Need for Living the Supernatural, Spirit-Filled Life

Despite the case for fully embracing the work of the Holy Spirit so far, there may yet be some objections to the working of the Holy Spirit. These objections will be dealt with in more detail in the next few chapters.

Holy Spirit to come—which is better for the believer!

Chapter 3: Evangelical Cultural Hindrances Regarding the Spirit

There are certain values or understandings agreed upon in the evangelical church that inform the culture and understanding of Evangelicals in such a way as to make it difficult for them to completely embrace the activity of the Holy Spirit in their midst. The values I want to discuss are as follows: the primacy of scripture (or Luther's *solo scriptura*)–only scripture can be trusted; the primacy of the cross, i.e., the cross is the best if not only focus of the Christian experience, and it enhances evangelism; personal experiences are unreliable in matters of the faith; and God prefers reverence in matters of worship. I will begin by addressing the church culture which consciously, if not subconsciously reinforces resistance to the Holy Spirit.[12] Afterward, we will

12 By culture I mean those influences that reinforce certain beliefs and behaviors as a result of association with a particular group of people. Sometimes these influences

look at more personal objections that are sometimes raised regarding the Holy Spirit working in the individual believer's life.

The Primacy of the Scripture: The Role of Texts (scripture) in the Early Church

For the first 20 years of the life of the church Christians relied upon the Holy Spirit and the testimony of believers, especially the apostles and eye witnesses who heard Christ teach and saw him minister. The compilation of the various letters and the formation of the gospels (biographies) were expedited by the need for instruction for new believers in territories beyond Palestine and to counteract the various heresies that began to emerge to taint the church. Prior to scriptural canonization, believers trusted the Holy Spirit and had only the Old Testament as their scripture. Thus, references to the value of scripture are contextualized in what may be regarded as the Old Testament. For example, 2 Timothy 3:16 states, "All Scripture is God-breathed and is useful for teaching, rebuking, correcting and training in righteousness, so that the man of God

---

may be methods, doctrines, nostalgic remembrances, parents and peers, and certain notions of security and ap-proval of others.

18

may be thoroughly equipped for every good work" is more of a reference to the Old Testament than it is to the writings which became the New Testament. Furthermore, Rev. 22:18-19 states, "I warn everyone who hears the words of the prophecy of <u>this book</u>: If anyone adds anything to them, God will add to him the plagues described in <u>this book</u>. And if anyone takes words away from this book of prophecy, God will take away from him his share in the tree of life and in the holy city, which are described in this book" is more a reference to the book of Revelation proper than a reference to the entire Bible or even the New Testament, which was in the process of being canonized. Jesus, the example of Christians, who is the fullest personification and application of the word of God, is the standard more so than a text. Jesus is the fullest revelation of God the Father. We must understand that the life of Christ is mediated by the scriptures inspired by the Holy Spirit through human instrumentality. The scriptures are trustworthy and infallible, but human interpretation of the scripture is not infallible. The privileging of the scripture is, in some ways, counter-productive to reliance on the Holy Spirit because of human interpretation.

Evangelical Cultural Hindrances Regarding the Spirit

The Privileging of Scripture Places the Text above God Himself

The privileging of the Scripture results in the deification of the Bible for many. For example, some evangelicals say that if an experience is not in the bible it is not legitimate. Such a position is spiritually harmful in a number of ways. First of all, God is greater and more expansive than any text could possibly convey. To equate the Bible with the concept of ultimate authority is to say that the Bible is God. God is not bound to the limitations of his own previously revealed word mediated through a culturally informed human agency. To suggest that God can only say what has said is to "mute" God and make him irrelevant. To challenge God himself using human understanding of his own word is presumptuous and places an individual into the role of the Pharisee. The Pharisees condemned Christ for breaking the Sabbath because of their understanding of the Sabbath and the addition of many laws governing it. Jesus said he was the Lord of the Sabbath. In other words, Jesus told those who held the "scripture" in the highest regard, that as God he could determine the nature of the Sabbath better than they. At issue was the Pharisees' unwillingness to change, to believe that God could send a messiah that didn't fit their doctrine. Their doctrine kept them from experiencing God and even caused them to fight against the very purposes of God. The scenario is familiar even today. Just as the Pharisees opposed Jesus, some evangelicals oppose the work of the Holy Spirit in ways that are not defined by doctrine. It is important to define the situation in this way, because evangelicals believe the Holy Spirit does have a ministry, albeit a more limited one.[13]

Secondly, a privileged text mediates and diverts the believer from having a direct experience with God (the Holy Spirit). Evangelicals find the static nature of the scripture comforting despite the fact that the scriptures have spawned, through human interpretation, diverse doctrines many contrary to each other. In the desire to avoid the supposed subjectivity of relying on the Holy Spirit, evangelicals must nevertheless rely on the Holy Spirit to negotiate the appropriate meaning of scripture. Ultimately, it is the Holy Spirit (the author of the text) who determines the meaning of the text beyond even

---

13 Evangelicals emphasize the regenerative and sanctifying work of the Holy Spirit. Thus, the Holy Spirit is primarily concerned with getting people saved and then helping them to obey the scriptures and manifest characteristics associated with Christ. Additionally, the Holy Spirit is seen as a guide to the scriptures in order to guarantee the correct interpretation.

cultural considerations and human invention. It would seem, like the children of Israel, some evangelicals would prefer to have the text [Moses and the law] mediate the awesome presence of God as revealed on the mountain (Exodus 20:18-21).[14]

The limitations of text, albeit a Holy Text, are seen in a number of ways. First, the reliance upon text has limited the manifest presence and grace of God available to the believer by imprisoning the interaction between the believer and God in an informational matrix. Second, believers access the scriptures by way of translation. Without an understanding of the original languages evangelicals must respond to meaning that has be invested in the English language that translates a language and culture that is not Western in origin. An examination of the Amplified Bible, which highlights the nuances

---

14 "When the people saw the thunder and lightning and heard the trumpet and saw the mountain in smoke, they trembled with fear. They stayed at a distance and said to Moses, "Speak to us yourself and we will listen. But do not have God speak to us or we will die. "Moses said to the people, "Do not be afraid. God has come to test you, so that the fear of God will be with you to keep you from sinning." The people remained at a distance, while Moses approached the thick darkness where God was" (Exodus 20:18-21).

of the original languages, illustrates the broad scope of meaning that translators must choose from. Additionally, understanding the scripture is dependent upon the inner matrix of associations the individual has generated by his or her own experiences.[15] Third, privileging text (scripture) results in prioritizing being "right" or doctrinally correct over one's relationship with God or his Spirit. Interestingly enough, a recent poll by the Barna Research group regarding those who hold most firmly to the fundamentals of the evangelical faith

---

15 The connection between language and meaning has been developed by literary theorists, rhetoricians and poststructuralists who have explored the imprecision and flux of language in terms of human communication. Bakhtin discusses the fact that the mere mention of the word chair to a group of people will generate a variety of mental pictures. Add to this mix, his social constructionist notion that it is impossible to be free from the constraints of language in its variegated forms and these forms have made "objective" analysis (a person without any bias) next to impossible problematizes any rote reliance on a text apart from the governing and interpretive voice of the Holy Spirit. The stronger the relationship a believer has with the Holy Spirit the more likely the correct interpretation. This tends to be denied by some evangelicals who believe education and rationalism is humanity's best interpretive hope.

yields a few surprises. The groups who statistically affirm doctrines of the faith dearest to evangelicals (resurrection, salvation by faith, etc) are not groups like the Baptists or Presbyterians (both text oriented groups) but other groups that emphasize the Holy Spirit. The top believing group statistically is The Assemblies of God. Non-denominational groups even score higher than the Baptists (data from Barna Research Group). The accusation that emphasizing the Spirit will lead to a non-biblical, subjective faith is groundless. If anything, those who rely on the Spirit the most heavily have a greater appreciation and application of the words of the bible compared to their "evangelical" counterparts.

In conclusion, the question is do you want a relationship with Jesus (God/Holy Spirit) or are you going to focus on having the right doctrine in order to objectify your relationship with Jesus. Some people elevate the bible to the position of God and then the Bible becomes the focus of the relationship to the exclusion of having an "experiential" relationship with Jesus/Holy Spirit. A relationship with the Bible is a mental/rational process that relies on the human mind for understanding. There is no connection of the heart or necessary reliance on the Holy Spirit. Christianity becomes a propositional (a belief) system instead of a relationship of devotion to the

24

"Living Word."

Emphasizing Jesus over the Holy Spirit promotes Evangelism

It has been the common claim of some evangelicals that the "baptism" with the Holy Spirit or any emphasis on the gifts of the Holy Spirit detracts from the important task of evangelism. Somehow the perspective of emphasizing "Jesus" over the Holy Spirit is seen as being more faithful to the cross and the "gospel" because the emphasis remains on the doctrine of salvation. Thus, certain evangelicals are guilty of creating a false dichotomy between two members of the Trinity. The fact remains that the greatest evangelistic harvest occurred at the coming of the Holy Spirit (Acts 2:1-4, 7-8, 16-17, 37, 41). In this case, tongues, which is an instrument of evangelism, is a phenomena that is roundly rejected by most evangelicals.[16] However, the fact remains

---

16 Evangelicals would argue that the tongues represented here are known languages and not ecstatic utterances as mentioned in 1 Corinthians, even though Paul states that tongues "are a sign, not for believers but for unbelievers" (1 Cor. 14:22). Nevertheless, most evangelicals would not find tongues acceptable in their worship sources regardless of the type. In fact, it would be assumed that no interpreter exists for such a practice and in truth they would be

that Jesus, himself, confirms the central role of the Holy Spirit in evangelism. He states, "When he comes, he will convict the world of guilt in regard to sin and righteousness and judgment" (John 16:8). The convicting of the heart of the unbeliever is the role of the Holy Spirit. Jesus also tells his disciples that the Holy Spirit would give them the words to say to those that oppose them. In fact, evangelism was not possible without the coming of the Holy Spirit. Jesus' admonition was that the disciples should wait on the Holy Spirit to cloth them with power from on high (Luke 24:49). This is reiterated by Luke when Jesus tells his disciples "But you will receive power when the Holy Spirit comes on you, and you will be my witnesses in Jerusalem, and in all Judea and Samaria, and to the ends of the earth" (Acts 1:8).[17]

---

correct. The gift of interpretation of tongues is predicated upon the acceptance and exercise of a tongue. Without the acceptance of the former there is little reason to believe the latter will develop.

17 It has been taught by some evangelicals that the coming of the Holy Spirit in the Book of Acts is the initiation of the church, i.e., the church was born and people became believers for the first time (indwelt by the Holy Spirit). This is incorrect. John 20:22 states, "And with that he breathed on them and said, 'Receive the Holy Spirit.'" The Greek tense of *lambano* (receive) is ingressive implying

An examination of incidents where the disciples were involved in testifying about Jesus is sometimes preceded by the phrase "being filled with the Holy Spirit." Peter, before testifying about Jesus was filled with the Holy Spirit: "Then Peter, filled with the Holy Spirit, said to them: 'Rulers and elders of the people!'" (Acts 4:8 NIV).

An examination of the martyr Stephen confirms that he was full of the Holy Spirit and witnessed in His power. However, the paramount example of biblical evangelism, other than Christ, is the evangelist Philip. Philip's brand of evangelism, which is common among Charismatic/Pentecostal-type evangelists, is most glaringly absent from those who limit the power of the Holy Spirit. Doubtless, some will remark "What about Billy Graham?" God bless him. He ministered in the Holy Spirit. So did John

---

that a foretaste or down payment of the Spirit was made. One might argue this represents the indwelling of the Holy Spirit for the disciples and the start then of the church. The language structure is similar to when God breathed into Adam the breath of life and it certainly is in keeping with the notion that the Spirit entered the disciples. The debate on this particular issue is beyond the scope and purpose of this chapter, but there is enough evidence to suggest that the Holy Spirit is undeniably connected to evangelism.

the Baptist (yet without miracles). Yet, Billy Graham's ministry is not the biblical prototype represented by the scripture. Am I saying, Billy Graham's ministry is unbiblical? No. Preaching the gospel is never unbiblical, but neither is healing the sick while you preach the gospel. No honest evangelical can dispute the fact that signs and wonders accompanied the preaching of the gospel in the ministry of Jesus, the disciples, and Philip, the evangelist. If you read Acts 8:4-8, 12 (Philip's evangelism crusade) you will find a picture of a crusade that is entirely different than a lot of evangelical crusades. Acts 8:4-8 reads:

> Those who had been scattered preached the word wherever they went. Philip went down to a city in Samaria and proclaimed the Christ there. [6] When the crowds heard Philip and saw the miraculous signs he did, they all paid close attention to what he said. With shrieks, evil spirits came out of many, and many paralytics and cripples were healed. So there was great joy in that city. . . . But when they believed Philip as he preached the good news of the kingdom of God and the name of Jesus Christ, they were baptized, both men and women.

28

There will be those who suggest that those days are over and we must rely on a gospel without miracles, because such miracles are no longer needed. Balderdash. I cannot go into the depth of the error of such thinking without diverting from the purpose of this chapter. Suffice it to say, the church needs the Holy Spirit and all he does as much today as ever, and certainly the circumstances around the world require the ministry of the Holy Spirit in evangelism.

Is it possible to evangelize while limiting the power ministry of the Holy Spirit? Yes. In order to minister without relying on the miraculous *power of the Holy Spirit* methods and strategies to break down the defenses of unbelievers must be utilized. Then, the gospel must be shared in a convincing way (usually involving a rational argument of some kind). Consequently, the church has devised every kind of method and strategy imaginable to reach the lost apart from the activities and gifts of the Holy Spirit portrayed in the scripture.

In one strategy, churches have tried to become culturally relevant to the lost. Thus, the rise of "seeker-sensitive" churches and the inclusion of "styles" within the context of the church (the rise of health/entertainment services, videos, Christian music set to secular styles etc.). The goal of this cultural accommodation is to make a lost person feel comfortable in the church, i.e., not to scare off the unbeliever. Apart from highly critical/judgmental people, who no one wants to affirm in the church anyway, the scariest thing that could happen to a lost person is that he or she could witness the power of the Holy Spirit. This is understandable. If the moving of the Holy Spirit scares believers it is only reasonable to understand it would scare unbelievers. But perhaps that is a scare that both believers and unbelievers need. When the Holy Spirit shows up, He demands to be Lord of every life and all that goes on. This is something both believers and unbelievers need to realize.

Those who have an honest heart for evangelism by excluding the working of the Holy Spirit as an expression of their church life and evangelism are doing a disservice to those whom they are trying to reach. It is not God's intention to accommodate himself to anyone—believer or unbeliever. To introduce a believer into a weakened, watered-down expression of Christian community life is deceptive and just a little bit patronizing. Perhaps, God doesn't need converts that bad if he has to work that hard to please them.[18]

---

18 A little bit of tongue-in-cheek sarcasm to make my

More importantly, the gospel that is being preached is not the "full gospel" (a term that is irksome to many evangelicals who feel like their gospel [good news] is as good as anyone else's). The good news (gospel) is not just that Jesus saves, but that he also heals, delivers from demons, and empowers believers with the Holy Spirit. The gospel in its totality is referred to as the "gospel of the kingdom." It is this gospel that Jesus both taught/preached and practiced (Acts 1:4, 10:38; Luke 4:18). However, for many evangelicals the so-called "hype of the Holy Spirit" is an embarrassment—"a three-ring circus" that is not "dignified"[19] However, the apostle Paul, who said the kingdom of God is not a

___

point. Clearly, God loves everyone, and it is His will that all should be saved. However, if the parable of Jesus and the rich young ruler means anything, it means that God does not accommodate sinners in their sin. Jesus drove away as many people as he attracted by his "hard sayings." Sinners must repent, not simply join the club. Feeling uncomfortable is part of the process of conversion. It is called "conviction" that leads to repentance. Doubtless, some will say, "Look at our results!" In response, I would say by their standard Jesus failed miserably. He died with few believing in him.

19 An attitude encountered from those who are used to a more sedate tradition of worship.

matter of talk but of power (1 Cor.4:20), said he was not ashamed of the gospel of Jesus Christ because it was the power of God unto salvation for all who believed (Romans 1:16). It is time for believers, and particularly evangelicals, to stop apologizing for the phenomenal work of the Holy Spirit.

Finally, since it is reasonable and biblical to assume that the Holy Spirit is integral in bringing unbelievers to repentance and salvation, it stands to reason the greater the manifest presence of the Holy Spirit, the greater the conviction and hence the greater the evangelistic effort.[20]

Personal Experience is Unreliable

Evangelicals claim that those who rely on their personal experience with the Holy Spirit rather than the authority of the scriptures are basing

---

20 While this is logically true, the governing factor, which determines result often times, is connected with the faith of the congregation and its leadership. In many evangelical congregations there is faith for conversions, but not faith for the other works. The Holy Spirit is willing to honor that kind of faith, as limiting as it may seem, but He will re-act differently if He and His work are disparaged by those same individuals.

their faith and argument on personal experience.[21] Because of the primacy given to the scriptures such an assertion seems weighty from a Western rhetorical perspective. Personal experience is deemed subjective while the scriptures are deemed objective, even though much of scripture is a record of the personal experiences of believers and God dealing with those believers to reveal His truth. Contentment is a Christian virtue that Paul mentions several times telling us "godliness with contentment is great gain"(1 Timothy 6:6). Thus, as believers we seek to be content because we recognize that this is the proper response of gratitude toward God regardless of our circumstances. However, how did Paul come to this understanding? Paul states in his letter to the Philippians that he LEARNED how to be content in whatever circumstances he experienced. Consequently, that which has become scripture to us, promoting a godly and an inspired virtue, began as an experience for Paul. While the scripture "validates" personal experience, i.e., affirming and authorizing the experience as being connected to a biblical truth, personal experience also validates scripture, i.e.,

---

21 Jack Deere states this is the main reason evangelicals are opposed to the Spirit. They have not had any personal experiences with Him.

testifies to the real world effects of the word of God applied to daily living.

This understanding about experience "validating" scripture bothers evangelicals because they see it as an attempt to make the scriptures relative to the personal experiences of an individual. What about the experiences of individuals who want to suggest God is not as good as the scripture clearly states that He is (The problem of evil)? We would say that the individual does not have the proper understanding about a fallen world and the nature of human freewill—both extremely biblical concepts and both experientially validating the truth of the scripture. In fact, in order to present the gospel to unbelievers, we frequently appeal to their experiences of "need/unhappiness" with their lives apart from Christ. We go on to suggest that receiving Jesus as their personal Savior will result in a change (new experience) in their personal lives. While there most certainly needs to be caution in this realm, evangelicals cannot have it both ways: affirming their personal experiences as being biblical, while denying the personal experiences of those who have clear support from scripture that their experiences are biblical. In short, the personal experiences of Charismatic-type Christians are validated by scripture, and their experiences testify (validate) what the scripture says is available to the Christian. How is it that the "lack of experience" in the things of the Holy Spirit is used to invalidate what the scripture says? Spoken succinctly, Charismatics testify about what they know experientially, while some evangelicals testify about what they don't know experientially.

John Wimber used to give an illustration about scuba diving. Which scuba diver would you trust to take you on your first underwater diving experience? One scuba diver has read all the books on scuba diving that are available and can quote from those books, "chapter and verse." Yet, he has never gone scuba diving even once. The other scuba diver has be diving thousands of times and has taken first time divers diving a high percentage of those times. He knows what it is like and has experienced all the possible pit-falls that may not even be mentioned in the books. He knows what the first-time diver is going to experience, what it feels like. Which diver would you go with on your first dive? Stated another way, would you prefer a newly graduated surgeon at the top of his class with only a few assists in the operating room, or an experienced surgeon with hundreds of successful surgeries, who has stayed current with the latest surgical techniques. Common sense tells us that the disparaging of personal experience is somehow flawed. As many new graduates are finding out, experience matters in the workplace and not just book-learning. Now, I have painted a false dichotomy/false dilemma to make a point. We need both. However, the Christian who has committed himself or herself to scripture and has the experiences to back it up is the one who is balanced, not the one who disparages experience in favor of doctrinal interpretation. The goal of the scriptures is to bring individuals into the experience that the scriptures record. No evangelical would be satisfied merely relying upon the record of what it takes to be saved without actually having "experienced" the salvation spoken of first-hand. Evangelicalism is built upon the notion that it is paramount that a person "experience salvation" personally. While "personal experience" (another name for one's "testimony") is heralded by evangelicals, those experiences not directly related to the notion of repentance/ conviction are received skeptically, if at all. In short, experiences already received by evangelicals are okay, while experiences that have not already been experienced are suspect. Thus, while charismatic Christians are accused of arguing from experience, evangelicals may be accused of arguing from a lack of experience.

For evangelicals, the comfort of their religious tradition, which emphasizes education and natural ability, is preferable to the unpredictability of relying on the Holy Spirit for ministry. This penchant for going with what you know is understandable when the option is laying down all your capabilities and what you currently know in order to explore the realm of the Holy Spirit's ministry. This process of surrender to the Holy Spirit is made more difficult for evangelicals because of some of the factors previously mentioned and some I will now relate: doctrinal tradition and church pragmatics.

Because of their reformed theological heritage that emphasizes the total depravity and sinfulness of the human condition, evangelicals do not trust themselves as vehicles of God's grace, i.e., cooperating partners in the ministry of Jesus by way of the Holy Spirit. This is why they have posited their trust in the scriptures (mentioned previously) and have avoided anything that seemed subjective (coming from a person) to them. Such a position is evidenced by the affirmation of prayer to a God that is "up there," instead of the ministry of laying on of hands, which emphasizes the God who dwells in the believer doing the work of Christ. Strangely, evangelicals sometimes feel like humans are somehow getting the credit of stealing God's glory if God uses them instead of answering prayer and doing it directly himself. This dichotomy is foreign to the New Testament because Jesus clearly intends for his disciples to do the same works he has been doing (John 14:11-12), and he is unconcerned about humans "stealing" God's glory, because God desires to share his glory freely.[22]

Evidence of this pattern of ministry (preference for distant prayer over the personal laying on of hands) may be observed in many evangelical prayer meetings (particularly traditional Baptists) where those suffering in the congregation are "lifted up" before the throne without any personal contact being made. In essence, the suffering saint is being talked about (prayed for) in the third person while he or she sits only a few feet away listening. The schema for such ministry goes something like this:

---

22 Jesus goes on to tell his disciples (apostles), "I tell you the truth, anyone who has faith in me will do what I have been doing. He will do even greater things than these, because I am going to the Father. And I will do whatever you ask in my name, so that the Son may bring glory to the Father. You may ask me for anything in my name, and I will do it" (John 14:12-14).

In regard to sharing God's glory, Jesus states that this is the purpose of God for believers. "All I have is yours, and all you have is mine. And *glory has come to me through them* [my emphasis]" (John 17:10). And, "I [Jesus] have given them the glory that you [God] gave me" (John 17:22).

the person praying shoots a request up to God who, in turn, makes a decision about answering the prayer. If He gives the green-light on the request, He does something from his headquarters in heaven. It should be mentioned that due to the sovereignty of God, believers are cautioned not to expect an answer right away or even believe that they will receive the desired result spoken in their request. Consequently, all parties involved are not really responsible for any of the outcome of the prayer. The faith of those praying and those prayed for is not a matter to be dwelt upon, nor is the possibility of personal sin connected to the one suffering a matter for concern. In the end, the ministry process, even when passionate, is somewhat clinical in the sense that everyone tends to feel like they are not an important part of the process. Believers don't touch each other, nor do they expect to see a solution to the problem right away. It is all up to God, and believers do not play a role in the process, because they are just sinners who are given no authority in the earth to act on behalf of God. God is sovereign, and he won't share his power with mere humans. How contrary to the word of God! "You shall receive power when the Holy Spirit has come upon you" (Acts 1:8a).

More nefarious to the above equation is the concern that those who would attempt to exercise

Evangelical Cultural Hindrances Regarding the Spirit

spiritual power will fall prey to some demonic influence. The imbalance in such a position is seen in various quarters of evangelical thinking. In fact, it may be said that the devil and his minions are seen as being more powerful than the working of the Holy Spirit in believers, despite the fact the scriptures declare "Greater is he [Holy Spirit] that is in you than he [Satan] that is in the world" (1 John 4:4). The exercise of the Holy Spirit's power through believers being attributed to demons is not a new accusation, and it is in keeping with an erroneous and heretical eschatological system known as dispensationalism.[23]

---

23 The Pharisees accused Jesus of casting out demons by the Spirit of Beelzebub. Luke 11:15-20 states: "But some of them said, 'By Beelzebub, the prince of demons, he is driving out demons.' Others tested him by asking for a sign from heaven. Jesus knew their thoughts and said to them: 'Any kingdom divided against itself will be ruined, and a house divided against itself will fall. If Satan is divided against himself, how can his kingdom stand? I say this because you claim that I drive out demons by Beelzebub. [19] Now if I drive out demons by Beelzebub, by whom do your followers drive them out? So then, they will be your judges. [20] But if I drive out demons by the finger of God, then the kingdom of God has come to you."

Dispensationalism, a recent end-times interpretive scheme, suggests that things are going to get worse and worse till Jesus returns and rescues a

40

This system posits authority only in an interpretation of the scripture that denies the signs and wonders performed in the apostolic age to the church today (called Cessationism). Therefore, if miracles do occur, it is most likely the devil is doing them. The false prophet of the book of Revelation uses signs to deceive people and Jesus rebukes those who seek after a sign.[24] Furthermore, the ability to do signs

---

beleaguered church (the rapture) so that he can get back to the real purpose God has upon his heart—the establishment of the Jewish nation. While there are many heretical aspects to Dispensationalism, the aspects that make it hard for evangelicals to accept the power ministry of the Holy Spirit deal with the closing of the age of miracles or the dispensation of the apostolic church age. Since God no longer works miracles through believers, it stands to reason if any miracles are done it must be of the devil, because it is said he would lead people astray through false signs and wonders. Revelation 13:13-14 states, And he [the false prophet] performed great and miraculous signs, even causing fire to come down from heaven to earth in full view of men. Because of the signs he was given power to do on behalf of the first beast, he deceived the inhabitants of the earth.

24 Undoubtedly there are those who would suggest that it is inappropriate to emphasize signs and wonders because Jesus said, "'A wicked and adulterous generation looks for a miraculous sign, but none will be given it except

and wonders apparently does not guarantee one has a personal relationship with Jesus Christ. Matthew 7:21-23 states,

---

the sign of Jonah.' Jesus then left them and went away" (Matt. 16:4). Such individuals should be intellectually and hermeneutically honest with the text. Jesus was speaking to the Pharisees and the Sadducees (a wicked generation) when he spoke these words to them. The Sadducees denied miracles and basically anything supernatural (today's liberals) and the Pharisees denied that anything was true regarding God that did not find its authorization in the Old Testament scriptures and rabbinic writings (today's fundamentalists). These two parties did not want to believe in Jesus. Their request for a miraculous sign was based on their unbelief, not on their willingness to receive Christ. Thus, they are wicked not because a miraculous sign is bad (Jesus affirmed miraculous signs in other contexts), but because they refused to believe in Christ and were putting God to the test in order to vindicate their unbelief. Jesus tells them the sign of Jonah would be given to them (they already disbelieved in Jesus on the basis of previous miracles he had performed), i.e., his resurrection. It is interesting to note that Jesus then later says that there would be those who would not believe even if the rich man escaped hell to warn his brothers (Luke 16:31--"He said to him, `If they do not listen to Moses and the Prophets, they will not be convinced even if someone rises from the dead.'"). Clearly, the demonic deception rests with those who would deny the ministry of the Spirit today, as it was denied by those who opposed Jesus in his day.

> Not everyone who says to me, 'Lord, Lord,'
> will enter the kingdom of heaven, but only
> he who does the will of my Father who is in
> heaven. Many will say to me on that day, `
> Lord, Lord, did we not prophesy in your
> name and in your name drive out demons
> and perform many miracles?' Then I will tell
> them plainly, `I never knew you. Away from
> me, you evildoers!

In this passage of scripture, it appears there are those who **claim [my emphasis]** Jesus as Lord, but they are not doing "the will of my [Jesus'] Father who is in heaven." As this is prior to the cross (atoning work) of Jesus and the regeneration of the Holy Spirit in the believer, the only connection with the earthly Christ is situated in obedience to the Father. In short, these individuals are NOT followers of Christ. This is established by Christ, who says "I never knew you" and his calling them "evil doers."

This passage, which is used to disparage Charismatics or those who emphasize the supernatural ministry of Jesus, by way of the Holy Spirit, suggests they are not Christians or believers. To say that those who claim Jesus as Lord and are obedient to the Father are not believers is the worst kind of pride and judgmentalism, violating Jesus' prayer for unity among believers (John 17:23).

Evangelical Cultural Hindrances Regarding the Spirit

Today's believers, who cast out demons, are "post" cross of Christ and regenerated by the Holy Spirit. They are known by Christ because they were sealed by the Holy Spirit, have their names written in the Lamb's Book of Life (Phil. 4:3 and Rev. 13:8), and they are "doing the will of the Father" according to the scripture and the words of Jesus—"cast out demons"(Luke 10:17). Additionally, the same passage can be rhetorically turned around and used against Cessationist, fearful evangelicals, who call Jesus Lord but do not "do the will of the Father by their refusal to obey the command of Jesus to "cast out demons."

Furthermore, prior to Jesus casting out demons, the Jews also cast out demons (Luke 11:19)[25] and they didn't know Jesus, nor did He know them. Jesus asked the Pharisees in whose name did their disciples cast out demons since they accused Him of casting out demons by Beelzebub (Lord of the Flies or Satan)—sound familiar?. Charismatics are accused of doing supernatural works under the influence of the demonic, just like their Lord Jesus. Nevertheless, there are Christians who do the will of God by casting

---

25 Luke 11:19 Now if I drive out demons by Beelzebub, by whom do your followers drive them out? So then, they will be your judges. 20 But if I drive out demons by the finger of God, then the kingdom of God has come to you.

44

out demons, and there are Jews that reject Jesus and cast out demons. Oddly enough, the only people who can't or won't cast out demons are those who deny the power of the Holy Spirit and the present ministry of Christ in the earth today.

From a theological viewpoint it is easy to see why evangelicals would not place their trust in supernatural phenomena. But then again, evangelicals are not being asked to put their trust in supernatural phenomena (at least not by those who truly know the Lord as he desires). Evangelicals are asked by Christ to put their trust in Him and in the Holy Spirit, which is the Spirit of Christ. The supernatural things that are done are not done by believers, per se, but by the Holy Spirit who lives in believers. It is God who does the work whether he does it from his throne in heaven or from the heart of the Christian.

In fairness, the gifts and ministry of the Holy Spirit are not a validation of a person's character. God will use people who do not have a good character or even know him to perform the miraculous. A film in the 1970s called *Marjo,* about a character of the same name, was produced by a Charlatan who duped Pentecostal Christians, making fun of them backstage before and after his services (for some reason, I was given the opportunity to see this film three times

45

in three different classes in seminary--hmm was someone trying to make a point?). Interviews with those who received miracles and salvation said it was not because of the so-called "healing-evangelist" but because of their faith and the power or the word of God and his Spirit.

Those who are involved in carrying out the command of Jesus to heal the sick are sometimes referred to by evangelicals as "healers," which implies they are doing the work themselves. Yet, when an evangelical leads a person to salvation they are not called "saviors." The fact of the matter is that the Holy Spirit is doing both works himself–healing and saving. Both require trust in him, not trust in the one who is being used to do the work. The fact that believers sin do not make them sinners (their nature has been changed), nor is sinless perfection required to operate in the spiritual gifts (a case in point–the Corinthian church).[26] The overbearing emphasis on the reformed notion of depravity of man apart from a strong emphasis on the sanctifying work of Christ hinders evangelicals from trusting the God who lives

---

26 2 Cor. 5:17 states, "If anyone is in Christ he is a new creature, the old [nature] has passed away all things have become new." Believers are "partakers of the divine nature." (2 Peter 1:4).

within them.[27]

For many evangelicals a reluctance to turn loose of what they have already realized in Christ is simply based upon the fact that they are happy with where they are. As believers, they are a part of a church that meets their needs, evangelizes the lost and teaches them. In essence, they are successful by the standard of their peers (those whom they care about) and the risk to mess it all up is too high. Why change a good thing that you know about for the promise of something better that you are not sure of. This is a psychologically convincing argument that is not based on logic, but experience. It is tantamount to saying—"if it ain't broke don't fix it." The problem is: all believers are broke and in the process of being

---

27 Part of this fear was accentuated by certain faith teachers who maintained, because of the Holy Spirit who lived in them, they were "little gods" with a little "g." This did not help evangelicals in becoming comfortable with the God (Holy Spirit) who lives in them. Instead, they attributed this facet of God's truth to a new age deception based on an unfortunate choice of words (doubtless a little humility and less presumption on the part of such speakers would have also helped). It did not help that these same faith leaders fashioned interpretations of the scripture that deviated from the logical sense of the scripture. Thus, the illogical notion of "wrong in a few points=wrong in all points."

fixed over time; it is called sanctification, and it is the work of the Holy Spirit. Furthermore, the evangelical church, as it currently exists today, is neither biblically the way it was in the first century nor is it the way God intends for it to be towards the last days of the end times. Ministry apart from the supernatural, manifest power of the Holy Spirit is a mixture of the flesh (education, talent, and personality) and a certain element of the Holy Spirit. The same holds true for charismatic or Pentecostal types that do not rely totally on the Holy Spirit. However, for those who are seeking the manifest presence of God such individuals are trying to be completely yielded vessels (trying to minimize the flesh) to the Holy Spirit. Who can fault them for their effort?

The greatest risk evangelicals run by seeking to live their lives by the book only, instead of by the Holy Spirit in conjunction with the book, is creeping religiosity, i.e., a reliance on human effort to achieve ministry ends. Paul particularly addresses this problem in several sections of his letter to the Galatians. In Galatians, human effort is defined as the mechanism of the law. You do what the Bible says because there is a reward connected to the effort. At face value there seems to be little wrong with that statement, and Spirit-oriented Christians would agree with the addition of one proviso: Allow the Holy

Spirit to work through you in order to successfully do what the Bible says and the reward and result will be greater. Paul says it this way, "Are you so foolish? After beginning with the Spirit, are you now trying to obtain your goal by human effort? . . . Does God give you his Spirit and work miracles among you because you observe the law (or in this case rote obedience to biblical injunction) or because you believe what you heard? (Gal. 3:3,5).[28] In order to point out the difference between those who live their religious life by the book and those who live their lives according to the Spirit, Paul develops a metaphor using Sarah and Hagar and their two sons—Isaac and Ishmael.

In a nutshell, Paul compares those who live according to the law as a son of a slave woman, Hagar. They are not free or the child of promise, but they do persecute Isaac who represents believers

---

28 At this point an evangelical would assume what they heard was simply a gospel similar to theirs and contrary to the Jewish code to which Paul is referring. Paul is referring to the Jewish code, but he did not preach or teach a powerless gospel. A reading of the book of Acts, concerning Paul's missionary journeys, refutes such a notion. Miracles were happening in the Galatian church. The only question was: Do you return to the more comfortable format of study and compliance of the scriptures or do you continue to pursue the vibrancy of the Holy Spirit.

who are free, have received the promise (of the Holy Spirit) and are "born by the power of the Holy Spirit" (Gal. 421-31). There seems to be a type of animosity that exists between the evangelical and Spirit-oriented churches. At least in part, this is due to the insinuation that evangelicals may be "second-class" or inferior examples of Christians. This scheme of he enemy is an effort to keep evangelicals from yielding to what they already have—the Holy Spirit. The suggestion that allowing the Holy Spirit more control of one's life will make you charismatic or Pentecostal is simply a denominational rhetorical ploy to maintain the status quo. The Holy Spirit cannot be co-opted by any denomination or movement. The terms no longer matter in this day and time.[29] Be evangelical AND be filled with the Holy Spirit. Be an empowered

---

29 Among many evangelicals who came into the power of the Holy Spirit during the mid-80s, and more recently, terms such as charismatic and Pentecostal seem inappropriate. These basically theologically reformed individuals find little correspondence to the theology of Pentecostalism, nor the influences of some of the charismatic teachers from the 70s onward. Peter Wagner called such individuals "Third Wave," but this was prior to the revivals that have taken place in Toronto and Pennsacola. At present there are no "titles" which seem appropriate, although Wagner and others are now talking about "apostolic movements."

Christian, regardless.

Finally, evangelicals may balk at pursuit of the Holy Spirit because of the history of turmoil associated with the coming of the Holy Spirit. Evangelicals remember the divisiveness of he charismatic movement and subsequent church and denominational fights over the influence of the Holy Spirit when He simply decides to show up. Fond relationships are sometimes broken and individuals can lose their career with the denomination. The Spirit-oriented church tends not to form a traditional denominational structure making it hard to find ministry employment. Those that are forced to leave the church face a bewildering array of non-denominational congregations. Those who stay in their denomination from that moment on are looked on with suspicion and are given few if any leadership roles in the church. At any rate, such individuals may come to be viewed as divisive within the traditional church structure. The heralded "decently and in order" is always predicated upon the religious traditions of the denomination as opposed to the order of the Holy Spirit. Spirit-oriented individuals can take comfort in the words of Jesus when he says,

> "Do not suppose that I have come to bring peace to the earth. I did not come to bring

peace, but a sword. For I have come to turn "a man against his father, a daughter against her mother, a daughter-in-law against her mother-in-law-- a man's enemies will be the members of his own household.' "Anyone who loves his father or mother more than me is not worthy of me; anyone who loves his son or daughter more than me is not worthy of me; and anyone who does not take his cross and follow me is not worthy of me. Whoever finds his life will lose it, and whoever loses his life for my sake will find it. "He who receives you receives me, and he who receives me receives the one who sent me. Anyone who receives a prophet because he is a prophet will receive a prophet's reward, and anyone who receives a righteous man because he is a righteous man will receive a righteous man's reward. (Matthew 10:34-41)

Clearly, dissension and division came about when Jesus (God and the Holy Spirit) sought to bring God's order to his people. In hindsight, the rest is glorious history. Is it worth pursuing God/Christ, via the Holy Spirit. Yes, sell all you have to purchase this pearl of great price.

Worship Services must be Reverent

One struggle Evangelicalism has with the Holy Spirit may be viewed against the backdrop of reverence and irreverence. Evangelicals, by tradition, have associated reverence (respect for God) with a certain stylistic worship preference. The "free for all" participation of charismatic worshipers and their style of worship is problematic for some evangelicals.[30]

It has been said that the Lord expects reverence in his house as a sign of respect for his majesty or being. Reverence in this sense is somehow meant as a posture towards the one for whom reverence is shown. In one sense, this is perfectly biblical as the Lord does require reverence as an act of worship. However, reverence has come to be

---

30 Many evangelicals have adopted a more robust worship service embracing multiple instruments and affirming personal worship practices including the raising of hands, shouting and in some causes controlled opportunity for dancing. However, for the most part, congregants are not roundly given *carte blanche* (unrestricted freedom) to exercise their gifting and they are usually discouraged from any activity, regardless of the Holy Spirit's prompting, whereby it may be said that they are "making a scene."

limited in its association with a certain demeanor or style. Hence, reverence is associated with order/rank, regular arrangement (peace and quiet, silence, peacefulness, harmony, tranquility; control, discipline.); dignity becomes worthiness (dignified behavior, respectful deportment, self-possession, solemnity, decorum; stateliness, lofty bearing, proud demeanor, impressiveness of character; majesty, augustness.), and silence. Thus, it may be said that irreverence is associated with spontaneity or inappropriateness, which is informal, unbecoming, inelegant, noisy or clamorous (active, stirring, lively, bustling, tumultuous, agitated, and excited). By most accounts, any Pentecostal type of worship would be considered irreverent compared to Methodist/Episcopal reverence in worship. The central question is: Has the church misunderstood the biblical kind of reverence that God requires by replacing it with a human tradition of reverence that may at times replace or oppose true reverence towards God. For example, let's examine a well-known incident between David and his wife Michel.

The Story of David's irreverent worship
In 2 Sam. 2:14-23,

"David, wearing a linen ephod, danced

54

before the LORD with all his might, while he and the entire house of Israel brought up the ark of the LORD with shouts and the sound of trumpets. As the ark of the LORD was entering the City of David, Michal daughter of Saul watched from a window. And when she saw King David leaping and dancing before the LORD, she despised him in her heart. They brought the ark of the LORD and set it in its place inside the tent that David had pitched for it, and David sacrificed burnt offerings and fellowship offerings before the LORD. After he had finished sacrificing the burnt offerings and fellowship offerings, he blessed the people in the name of the LORD Almighty. Then he gave a loaf of bread, a cake of dates and a cake of raisins to each person in the whole crowd of Israelites, both men and women. And all the people went to their homes. When David returned home to bless his household, Michal daughter of Saul came out to meet him and said, "How the king of Israel has distinguished himself today, disrobing in the sight of the slave girls of his servants as any vulgar fellow would!" David said to Michal, "It was before the LORD, who chose me rather than your father or anyone from his house when he appointed me ruler over the LORD's people Israel--I will celebrate before the LORD. I will become even more undignified than this, and I will be humiliated in my own eyes. But by these slave girls you spoke of, I will be held in honor." And Michal daughter of Saul had no children to the day of her death.

Here we understand that reverence is the recognition of the Lordship of God; He is worthy and we are not. David rejects the idea that he must act in any way that would affirm his standing in the eyes of people. He desires to be less dignified if God would appear to be more dignified, i.e., greatly worshiped. David's reverence for God, dancing in inelegant, informal attire (half naked) is considered irreverence or undignified by Michel, who according to human tradition is the epitome of reverential and dignified demeanor. God affirms David, and, according to the story, it is Michel who forfeits intimacy because of her actions—it is recorded that she never bore David any more children.

Reverence Biblically Defined

If reverence is not a style or demeanor, what is it? At the heart of reverence is fear or awe.

The Hebrew word: Revere *(yare'* or *yaw-ray*)---a primitive root; means the following - fear 188 times, afraid 78 times, or terrible 23 times. The Greek New Testament words (from Vines) *entrepo* denotes respect or reverence and the word *eulabeia* has a similar meaning of reverence.

There is also an interesting occurrence of reverence that is connected to the concept of Lordship. There is a Hebrew word for reverence connected with the term *adodone* or *'adon,* which means lord. To revere something is to make it or him Lord. [31] While the word reverence may extend to earthly creatures, its association with God should give us pause. *Adonai* is used in association

---

31 firm, strong, lord, master 1a) lord, master;1a1) reference to men;1a1a) superintendent; of household, of affairs; 1a1b) master; 1a1c) king 1a2) reference to God; 1a2a) the Lord God; 1a2b) Lord of the whole earth; 1b) lords, kings; 1b1) reference to men;1b1a) proprietor of hill of Samaria; 1b1b) master; 1b1c) husband; 1b1d) prophet; 1b1e) governor; 1b1f) prince;1b1g) king 1b2) reference to God; 1b2a) Lord of lords (probably = "thy husband, Yahweh");1c) my lord, my master 1c1) reference to men; 1c1a) master; 1c1b) husband; 1c1c) prophet; 1c1d) prince; 1c1e) king; 1c1f) father; 1c1g) Moses; 1c1h) priest; 1c1i) theophanic angel; 1c1j) captain; 1c1k) general recognition of superiority; 1c2) reference to God; 1c2a) my Lord, my Lord and my God 1c2b) Adonai (parallel with Yahweh)

with *Yahweh* as a parallelism of Lord God. Thus, to reverence something or someone is to assign it a level of respect bordering on fear and awe consistent with the attribution of Lordship to that object of reverence. So there is a better definition available: to reverence God is to acknowledge his lordship over your life with the appropriate recognition of his awesome power and majesty. To know the "fear of the Lord" is to be brought to a place of reverence. Reverence is not a style or demeanor, but an attitude of the Heart that recognizes God (Christ or the Holy Spirit's lordship) over one's life. Thus, reverence can be shown in the midst of commotion.

For example, I have been in meetings where people were screaming, crying, laughing, shaking, jerking etc. In these meetings, the sense and feeling I received was one of "the fear of the Lord." In short, it was the Mount Sinai experience where God in essence "acted out." This commotion seems to be chaos for some, but it is God breaking through human order in order to assert his divine order-His Lordship. It is a fearful thing to lose control of yourself or even the control of a service, but the central issue is the Lordship of Jesus Christ over his people.

If reverence is fear and obedience to the Lordship of the Trinity, then irreverence is the refusal to obey or acknowledge the will and lordship of the

Trinity. Thus, those who refuse to submit to the Holy Spirit or honor his work among believers are the ones who are truly irreverent, not those who violate a human standard or style of reverence. It should be noted that heaven is a noisy place. It is so noisy that silence in heaven for a space of 30 minutes is recorded as noteworthy (Rev. 8:1).

Irreverence as an alternative

Having established the role of lordship assigned to reverence, certain things deserve irreverence. What are those things? Anything that makes a pretentious claim to lordship is questionable. For example, I am irreverent towards claims that trees and earthworms are as precious a life form as humans. Jesus himself said we are more important than donkeys rescued on the Sabbath. Let's face it, certain things are worthy of irreverence. For me, pretentious and self-absorbed people are worthy of irreverence if not the fan clubs and groupies that follow them. It stands to reason if there is someone worthy of reverence, there is someone worthy of irreverence. God will not allow himself to be a part of any set (category). He is the lone, one and only, revered one. Doesn't this lead to wholesale disrespect? It would if we did not recognize the Jesus who lives, speaks and does his work through us. We are called to respect one another, to love the Jesus in one another. Yet at the same time we should not be a part of affirming those who would have God's glory for only themselves.

How did reverence as a style become the norm?

"Style reverence" is based on religion or the idea that one must act a certain way in order to gain God's favor. It is the parent tugging on a noisy child's ear in church. It is the admonition to be good in church that we grew up with. It is the concept that one must stay orderly in ones' place and be a good foot soldier and not question orders. It is the same notion that suggests that "cleanliness is next to godliness." It is the human attempt to place God in the highest place by becoming a silent respectful platform for his being, as if God could not be God in any greater forum. It is the cry of the Pharisees that admonished Jesus to make his supporters be quiet at his triumphal entry. Jesus said if they stopped praising, the stones themselves would cry out.

Style reverence is not bad if we fall silent under his awesome presence, but it is just a religious formula if we believe God prefers it over anything else. A reading of the Psalms suggests that God actually prefers tumultuous praise over polite congratulations.

CHAPTER FOUR: BINARIAN OR TRINITARIAN: WHY THE HOLY SPIRIT IS JESUS TO US

It is not uncommon among Evangelicals to hear them offer thanks to "God and to our savior" without giving it a second thought that the Holy Spirit is a part of that Trinitarian equation. It is a common practice to omit references to the Holy Spirit in prayer. Furthermore, Evangelicals, while they will publicly express their love for God and Jesus, mentioning both by name, rarely do you hear them publicly tell the Holy Spirit that they love Him. It is like: Jesus points to the Father and the Holy Spirit points to Jesus, so there is no one left in the Trinity to point to the Holy Spirit. However, Jesus endorsed the Holy Spirit and his coming and suggested he was "another of the same kind." But isn't it true that the Father endorsing Jesus (This is my son in whom I am well pleased) is pointing to Christ just as Jesus is pointing to (endorsing) the Holy Spirit. Jesus said, "He who

61

acknowledges me, acknowledges the Father; He who denies me, denies the Father." This seems like an endorsement of the Trinity—when you've seen me you have seen the Father.[32] In other words, Jesus is saying that He reveals the Father in his own person (Hebrews 1:1-2), yet Paul says in 1 Corinthians that the Spirit knows God and reveals him to us. The Holy Spirit is the Spirit of Truth, who conveys to us the words of Jesus (he does not speak on his own)[33], but didn't Jesus say the same thing about himself when he said, "My words are not my own, they belong to the Father. I merely say what the Father is saying." [34]

---

32 John 14:8-9a Philip said, "Lord, show us the Father and that will be enough for us." [9] Jesus answered: "Don't you know me, Philip, even after I have been among you such a long time? Anyone who has seen me has seen the Father."

33 John 16:13-15 [13] But when he, the Spirit of truth, comes, he will guide you into all the truth. He will not speak on his own; he will speak only what he hears, and he will tell you what is yet to come. [14] He will glorify me because it is from me that he will receive what he will make known to you. [15] All that belongs to the Father is mine. That is why I said the Spirit will receive from me what he will make known to you."

34 John 7:16-17 [16] Jesus answered, "My teaching is not my own. It comes from the one who sent me. [17] Anyone who

And yet Jesus is honored for speaking the words of the Father, but why isn't the Holy Spirit honored for speaking the words of Jesus? They all speak with the same voice. If they are the same in their "godness," and the message is the same, why isn't the Holy Spirit honored equally? Furthermore, Jesus said it was better for him to go away so that the Holy Spirit could come.[35] Someone better for us than Jesus!? In fact, Jesus declared those disciples he trained in supernatural ministry-- who actually did the works he did-- should wait until they received power from on high. "You will receive power when the Holy Sprit has come upon you to be my witnesses . . ." (Acts 1:9a). The Holy Spirit gave believers something that Jesus himself could not give, and they were told to wait for Him. This is the reason Jesus said, "I came to send fire [the Holy Spirit] on the earth, and how I

---

chooses to do the will of God will find out whether my teaching comes from God or whether I speak on my own. And John 5:19 [19]Jesus gave them this answer: "Very truly I tell you, the Son can do nothing by himself; he can do only what he sees his Father doing, because whatever the Father does the Son also does.

35 John 16:7 "But very truly I tell you, it is for your good that I am going away. Unless I go away, the Advocate will not come to you; but if I go, I will send him to you."

wish it were already kindled. But I have a baptism to undergo, and what constraint I am under until it is completed!"(Luke 12:49-50). What He is saying is that his purpose of being on the earth was so that he could die on the cross in order for the Holy Spirit to come. This may be a shock to those who only quote the verse out of John 3:17 where Jesus said he came to seek and save the lost. There seems to be a larger purpose than just salvation. Additionally, the apostle John said, "For this reason was the son of God manifest [appeared] to destroy the work of the evil one. (1 John 3: 8b--The reason the Son of God appeared was to destroy the devil's work.) Once again, his coming is more than just about evangelism. In regard to the Holy Spirit's coming, John the Baptist said of Jesus: "He will baptize you with the Holy Spirit and with fire" (Matthew 3:11b). Jesus also teaches his disciples to ask for the Holy Spirit in his discourse about a good father giving his children what they need. "Which of you fathers, if your son asks for a fish, will give him a snake instead? Or if he asks for an egg, will give him a scorpion? If you then, though you are evil, know how to give good gifts to your children, how much more will *your Father in heaven give the Holy Spirit to those who ask him!*"[my emphasis] (Luke 11:11-13). This is Jesus telling the disciples to ask the Father for the Holy Spirit.

If that is not enough, Jesus tells the Pharisees that they can blaspheme his name or insult him and be forgiven, but if they insult or blaspheme the Holy Spirit, they will not be forgiven in this age or the age to come because they committed an eternal sin (Luke 8:12-10; cp. Mark 3:28)-- "²⁸ Truly I tell you, people can be forgiven all their sins and every slander they utter, ²⁹ but whoever blasphemes against the Holy Spirit will never be forgiven; they are guilty of an eternal sin." It seems that Jesus is especially protective of the Holy Spirit. What has changed? Paul in two different letters tells believers to "not to grieve the Spirit" (Ephesians 4:30 "And do not grieve the Holy Spirit of God, with whom you were sealed for the day of redemption.") and in another letter to "not quench the Spirit (1 Thessalonians 5:19 "Do not quench the Spirit."). This suggests that you can suppress the influence of the Holy Spirit in yourself and in a congregation. This also occurs when you desire to trust yourself and do things your own way. Paul states that he puts "no confidence in the flesh" (Phil. 3:3). This is living life in one's own soul power. In essence, you are rebelling against the Lordship of Jesus/Holy Spirit. It is insulting the Spirit of Grace by telling the Holy Spirit you know better than He does regarding the desires of Christ and how He does his work.

The missing Dimension of Sanctification/Spiritual Formation - By Works or the Spirit?

In 2 Cor. 3:17-18, Paul compares the ministry (covenant) of the Spirit with the Old Testament covenant of Moses, suggesting that the covenant of the Spirit is far greater than that old covenant. In essence, this is a chapter about the Holy Spirit and how He reveals Christ to those who believe. In this passage, Paul connects the Holy Spirit with Jesus and suggests how the Holy Spirit enables us to become more like Jesus. If Jesus is going to rule His church--His body-- then the Holy Spirit is going to have to rule in the church. It is the knowledge of the unconditional love of Jesus that fortifies our obedience to the Lordship of Jesus, and yet the Holy Spirit is the Lord." **Now the Lord [Jesus] is the Spirit [Holy Spirit], and where the Spirit of the Lord is, there is freedom**. [my emphasis] [18] And we all, who with unveiled faces contemplate the Lord's glory, are being transformed into his [Jesus'] image with ever-increasing glory, which comes from **the Lord, who is the Spirit**"(2 Cor. 3:17-18). To have intimacy with Jesus you must have intimacy with the Holy Spirit, who is the life of Jesus in the earth and in you. This intimacy involves all aspects of our being and is much more than mental/rational assent to a doctrine. The Holy Spirit is a person, not a gift, a force, an endowment, a badge of spirituality or a substance that can be quantified. His life represents the life of

Jesus in us, so much so that the Holy Spirit is not just called the Spirit of God, but also the Spirit of Christ. In Romans 8:9-10, Paul states, [9] "You, however, are not in the realm of the flesh but are in the realm of the Spirit, if indeed the Spirit of God lives in you. And if anyone does not have the **Spirit of Christ**, they do not belong to Christ. [10] But if Christ is in you, then even though your body is subject to death because of sin, the Spirit gives life because of righteousness." Clearly, the bodily resurrected Christ who sits on the throne and is retained in heaven until his second coming is not the one who is in us; it is the Holy Spirit, and yet, it is Christ in us. It's a Trinity thing, hard to understand and even harder to explain. So, if you want Jesus to be Lord of your life and the church where you are in community, then the Holy Spirit is going to have to be Lord of both. This means the Holy Spirit is actively involved in leading us, and we need to be engaged in understanding what He is like as a person. To intimately know the Holy Spirit is to intimately know Jesus. You do not have intimacy with Jesus through head knowledge of the bible, but through devotional experience with Jesus by way of the Holy Spirit. While the wisdom of God/Christ is recorded in the New Testament, the guidance can also come from the person of the Holy Spirit. In Romans 8:14, it states, "For those who are led by the

The missing Dimension of Sanctification/Spiritual Formation - By Works or the Spirit?

Spirit of God are the children of God." Paul states, "if we are led by the Spirit we fulfill the law (Gal.5:18). He also says if we are led by the Spirit we will not fulfill the desires of the flesh (Gal.5:16). It is essential to understand that the Holy Spirit is a person who has feelings, thoughts, and motion. He is Jesus in the earth and in you. Your relationship with Jesus is bonded in your relationship with the Holy Spirit. Just like the scripture states, "Whoever **acknowledge**s me before others, I will also **acknowledge** [my emphasis] before my Father in heaven." (Matt. 10:32) Also, 1 John 2:23 states, "No one who denies the Son has the Father; whoever **acknowledges** [my emphasis] the Son has the Father also." This means the Jews who worship God but reject Jesus do not *have* the Father. Makes you wonder what happens if you deny the Holy Spirit. We don't have to wonder. Non-Trinitarian cults who deny the deity of Jesus, by necessity, de-personalize the Holy Spirit. However, sometimes we de-personalize the Holy Spirit by focusing on how he is an endowment within us (a gift or one of our spiritual abilities) or a substance/power (like an anointing). Even worse, He becomes the subject of some doctrinal dispute or a simple matter of study: pneumatology.

You can be embarrassed by, or refuse to stand up for, the Holy Spirit. "If you are ashamed of me before men, I will be ashamed of you before my Father in heaven."[36] When you were dating your intended, do you think you would be married today if you let her know that you did not want to be seen with her in public? Would any date, or relationship, go well if that was your attitude? Embarrassment regarding the Holy Spirit or a refusal to acknowledge Him in church is a similar attitude. We simply must become more intimate with the Holy Spirit and appreciative of His ministry, if we want to honor Jesus and, consequently, the Father. More importantly, for our sake, the Holy Spirit is the one who sanctifies and conforms us to the image of Christ. Our spiritual growth is dependent upon His working in us, as we shall see in the next chapter.

---

36 Luke 9:26 "Whoever is ashamed of me and my words, the Son of Man will be ashamed of them when he comes in his glory and in the glory of the Father and of the holy angels."

CHAPTER FIVE: THE MISSING DIMENSION OF SANCTIFICATION SPIRITUAL FORMATION - BY WORKS OR THE SPIRIT?

The funny thing about getting saved is no one actually tells you what you can do with yourself in order to grow spiritually, without having to work at it. This is a problem because Paul said in Colossians 2:6, "As you received Christ so walk in Him." I received Christ as someone who was lost and without hope, acknowledging there was nothing I did that could please God or earn his favor. Then after I was saved, I was told that I needed to read the word, pray, evangelize, go to church, and be a good steward of my money in order to grow spiritually and become a good Christian. This seemed reasonable because I was told that Jesus did all this (salvation by Him dying on the cross) for me, so in gratitude I ought to do all the things the church said for Him because that would please him. In essence, he loved me unconditionally when I was bad, but now that I am his child He loves me conditionally, i.e., if I do everything He commanded. It doesn't take long to figure out it is better to be loved unconditionally, than to be loved conditionally. Clearly, it is more fun to be the prodigal son at the party than the elder son in the field. And yet, many Christians feel like the elder son, overworked for Jesus and needing a "sin vacation"—a break from religious duties to be able to do whatever they want to do. For many, reading the bible is taxing if not unfruitful, and a "quite time" with Jesus is nothing more than a forced, dutiful habit. Don't get me wrong; the Christian disciplines are meant to provide God the opportunity to connect with our hearts. However, what if our hearts are cold and dry toward God? This kind of soil is not ready to receive from God. So the question remains: How are the motivations of the heart affected by God in such a way that it leads to a transformation in relationship with Him resulting in spiritual growth into the image of Jesus?

Part of the problem for evangelicals is the emphasis on salvation leads them to associate the ministry of the Holy Spirit simply with redemption. He is necessary to get people saved, but other than being a house guest (Jesus lives in my heart), he doesn't seem to have a lot to do in regard to spiritual

71

formation. Sure he is involved in the spiritual disciplines when we seek and yield to his influence, but how does the Holy Spirit actually conform our hearts to the image of Christ? What is this ministry of Sanctification?

According to the Greek language, sanctification is the process of being made holy and set apart for God's purposes. Theologians attribute this specific work to the Holy Spirit, much like the work of justification is attributed to the work of Christ on the cross. If we do not allow the Holy Spirit to bring transformation to us, we will gravitate toward religion, a plan of behavior modification based on adherence to a set of rules or principles to live by. These principles seem like they would be effective for helping us reach spiritual maturity, but they were not effective for the Jews who had perfected "holiness" through an entire system of laws (principles). However, Jesus confronts the best examples of the system (the Pharisees) and calls them white-washed tombs full of dead man's bones."Woe to you, teachers of the law and Pharisees, you hypocrites! You are like white washed tombs, which look beautiful on the outside but on the inside are full of the bones of the dead and everything unclean (Matthew 23:27). What didn't work for the Jews, does not work for Christians, as well. Paul addresses the pointlessness of trying to engage in self-reformation in several of his epistles. In Galatians 2:21, Paul states the law (keeping rules) cannot justify a person: "I do not set aside the grace of God, for if righteousness could be gained through the law, Christ died for nothing!" Furthermore in Colossians 2:22-23, Paul discourages Christians from relying on these rules in order to gain righteousness:"These rules, which have to do with things that are all destined to perish with use, are based on merely human commands and teachings. [23] Such regulations indeed have an appearance of wisdom, with their self-imposed worship, their false humility and their harsh treatment of the body, but **they lack any value in restraining sensual indulgence**" [my emphasis]. Paul, in fact, suggests that the Galatians were bewitched--under the spell of a demonic power--by those who wanted them to go back under the law:

> You foolish Galatians! Who has bewitched you? Before your very eyes Jesus Christ was clearly portrayed as crucified. [2] I would like to learn just one thing from you: Did you receive the Spirit by the works of the law, or by believing what you heard? [3] Are you so foolish? **After beginning by means of the Spirit, are you now trying to finish by means of the flesh?** [my emphasis]. [4] Have you

> experienced so much in vain—if it really was in vain? [5] So again I ask, does God give you his Spirit and work miracles among you by the works of the law, or by your believing what you heard? [6] So also Abraham "believed God, and it was credited to him as righteousness. (Galatians 3:2-6)

Paul states that the beginning work of the Holy Spirit should continue without impedance from human fleshly effort. "In the flesh" simply implies acting out of one's natural proclivities or human effort apart from the activity of the Holy Spirit. Sadly, some individuals act "in the flesh" when they are supposedly influenced by the Holy Spirit. It is possible that the Holy Spirit gets blamed for all kinds of "kookiness." However, the people who judge these individuals are just as much "in the flesh" as those whom they judge. For example, some believe that the Holy Spirit should be balanced with the scripture. The reason for this is the mistrust of "spiritual" experiences. They want to judge whether or not an experience is actually legitimate or merely an emotional expression of "the flesh." However, they are using their mind (personal interpretation of the bible) and their own personal experiences to judge the activity of the Holy Spirit or other believers; neither is advisable.

Relying on "the flesh" is an exercise in control through the use of mental or rational processes. This is the core of religion: man's attempt to find acceptance from God through human effort. Once again, the closest example of religion to Christianity is the Pharisee's version of Judaism. The religion/ legalism of the Pharisees has several consequences: 1. A focus on behavior and not on the attitude of the heart; 2. By extension, an external focus on behavior will lead to a kind of spiritual nit-picking where the more weightier issues of the heart are never addressed, which is what God is most concerned with; 3. Legalism leads to "performance orientation" which causes people to believe they have to earn God's acceptance and love; 4. Legalism violates the dynamics necessary for any relationship. None of these things help a believer get closer to God or result in becoming more like Christ. You do not have intimacy with Jesus simply by focusing on behavior/ obedience apart from a loving devotion of the heart. You must believe that Jesus loves you unconditionally even when you feel like circumstances suggest otherwise. You must love Jesus unconditionally, just like He loves you, and not just love Him when you feel like He is meeting your expectations.

The key to spiritual formation rests in the ability of a person to receive from God the things needed: including the fruit of the Holy Spirit; his gifts in us (1 Cor. 12:7-11)[37], his fruit (character)(Gal. 5:22-23)[38]; his revelation and power (Eph. 1:17-19)[39], even God's love (Eph. 3:16-19).[40]

---

37 Now to each one the manifestation of the Spirit is given for the common good. [8] To one there is given through the Spirit a message of wisdom, to another a message of knowledge by means of the same Spirit, [9] to another faith by the same Spirit, to another gifts of healing by that one Spirit, [10] to another miraculous powers, to another prophecy, to another distinguishing between spirits, to another speaking in different kinds of tongues, and to still another the interpretation of tongues. [11] All these are the work of one and the same Spirit, and he distributes them to each one, just as he determines.

38 But the fruit of the Spirit is love, joy, peace, forbearance, kindness, goodness, faithfulness, [23] gentleness and self-control. Against such things there is no law.

39 I keep asking that the God of our Lord Jesus Christ, the glorious Father, may give you the Spirit of wisdom and revelation, so that you may know him better. [18] I pray that the eyes of your heart may be enlightened in order that you may know the hope to which he has called you, the riches of his glorious inheritance in his holy people, [19] and his incomparably great power for us who believe.

40 [16] I pray that out of his glorious riches he may strengthen you with power through his Spirit in your inner being, [17] so

CHAPTER SIX: INCORRECT THINKING ABOUT THE HOLY SPIRIT

Sometimes the Holy Spirit and his activities are conflated with the reactions and consequential response of individuals who are encountering His ministry for the first time or in special circumstances. Those who are representatives of the "spirit-filled" life and ministry may not best convey the heart and priorities of the Holy Spirit. However, the reaction to such excesses can equally be misguided.

Tiered Christianity

In the past, evangelicals have resented the notion that somehow Charismatics or even Pentecostals felt they had a special relationship

---

that Christ may dwell in your hearts through faith. And I pray that you, being rooted and established in love, [18] may have power, together with all the Lord's holy people, to grasp how wide and long and high and deep is the love of Christ, [19] and to know this love that surpasses knowledge— that you may be filled to the measure of all the fullness of God.

with God that the evangelicals didn't have or could share. To counteract the often-times arrogance of some who would look down on evangelicals as being "unanointed," evangelicals declared they received everything they needed from God when they got saved. The end result was there was nothing more to be gained. This is, sadly, an erroneous and tragic view because God is not a respecter of persons and would freely give to any believer a greater sense of his presence and power. The important part of this discussion pertains to our own feelings about the work of the Holy Spirit in our midst. Invariably, there will be those whom God will touch in an overt or strong fashion. Others may have a milder experience and wonder why they did not have the same kind of experience as someone else. As Paul would say, when you compare yourself against someone else you are not wise (2 Cor. 10:12). The central issue is not your current experience, but whether you are willing to "go on" with God. If you are not receiving the desired result, don't withdraw in your spirit from pursuit of God. Love Him. For some, the wild excesses of those who rely on the Holy Spirit mean that there must be a balance to check the experiences of the Holy Spirit. In essence, the Holy Spirit should act in an orderly or reasonable way.

The Strange Doctrine of Moderation.

Steeped in the Western rationalism, founded upon the Aristotelian concept of "the golden mean," Christians sometimes believe that it is better to have a balanced life or a balanced approach to the Christian life in regard to the Holy Spirit's activity. This is expressed in a number of ways. While there is an element of wisdom in such counsel (there is such a thing as seasons, for example), nevertheless such common sense counsel is sometimes given to moderate (stifle) individuals in their radical pursuit of God. While drinking too much wine may lead to headaches, vomiting and a loss of consciousness, or over indulgence (lack of moderation), in regard to the Holy Spirit, there are no such side effects. The pop cultural criticism of "so heavenly minded that he is no earthly good" is a similar example/criticism by those who take umbrage with those who seem "too spiritual." Unfortunately, the paradigm of reasoning is eschewed. Does one balance the spiritual life with living a worldly life? No. Does one balance intimacy with Jesus with church programs, familial responsibilities, and practical service to God as if the Holy Spirit is somehow a separate component to be balanced against these other activities? No. Still there is a subtle need in Christendom to mitigate experiences with the Holy Spirit with other factors.

79

Incorrect Thinking about the Holy Spirit

For example, some believe that the Holy Spirit should be balanced with the scripture. Some have the creative approach of suggesting that the Christian should balance their lives utilizing the Trinity—Father (good government), the Son (scripture) and the Holy Spirit (spiritual experience). Despite the seeming common-sense that is attached to this approach, nevertheless the concept is marred at a few junctures. First, the arbitrator that keeps everything in balance is the human mind fortified by the human will. To pit the Holy Spirit against the scripture in some check and balance system usually results primarily in positing distrust in the direction of the Holy Spirit. This is an odd activity since the Holy Spirit is the author of the scriptures. Groups who are cautious of the influence of the Holy Spirit are fond of using their "tradition" of scriptural interpretation as a criterion for judging the Holy Spirit and his activity. One wonders if such individuals would dare ask the Holy Spirit to enlighten and correct their doctrine. Second, this approach suggests that the persons of the Trinity might be in disagreement with each other and shows a fundamental misunderstanding about the nature of the Trinity. Finally, the Trinity is conflated or made synonymous with human expression, which is flawed at best. How is human government the same as God's government? How is the full expression of the life of Jesus reduced to the few things that were actually recorded about Him in scripture? How is the life and expression of the Holy Spirit synonymous with the variegated spiritual experiences of individuals? This "balancing act" only makes sense if a person is primarily acting in their own flesh, which is what we are told not to do.

Clearly, or for some not so clearly, there is a conflating of the activity of the Holy Spirit and the exercising of the flesh. Scriptural admonition and guidance is certainly necessary to restrain the inappropriate exercise of the flesh. However, the Holy Spirit does not need the restraint and, in fact, He is essential in helping restrain the exercise of the flesh. The answer to fleshly excess is not opposition to the Spirit, but an actual increase and reliance on the Holy Spirit. One might add that resistance to the activity of the Holy Spirit is as much an exercise of the flesh as the hype or excess associated with the ministry of the Holy Spirit by believers who are exercising their flesh. It is true that the Holy Spirit is offensive to some. He offends religious people, demons, and those who mistrust or deny the supernatural. For others, the Holy Spirit is just too divisive.

The Holy Spirit is offensive

This view is generally a concern for those

who are trying to build unity among the various groups representing the Christian faith. Like the aforementioned quest for moderation, there is a desire to remove the more radical, and hence unpredictable, influences of the Holy Spirit in His manifold operations in order to promote unity or not to offend others. Unfortunately, the Holy Spirit is the only true source of unity in the Body. Psalm 133 is a psalm about unity which speaks of both the **oil** of anointing on Aaron's beard and the **dew** on Mt. Hermon (my emphasis--symbols of the Spirit). It begins by saying "How good and pleasant it is for brothers to dwell together in unity it is like . . . [anointing oil and dew]. The Holy Spirit doesn't divide. The Holy Spirit instead forces the issue of choosing who or what will be the real passion of the believer's heart. If the Holy Spirit offends, He offends the flesh. Jesus spoke of Matthew 10:34-38 states:

> [34] "Do not suppose that I have come to bring peace to the earth. I did not come to bring peace, but a sword. [35] For I have come to turn
> "'a man against his father, a daughter against her mother, a daughter-in-law against her mother-in-law—[36] a man's enemies will be the members of his own household.'
> [37] "Anyone who loves their father or mother more than me is not worthy of me; anyone

82

> who loves their son or daughter more than
> me is not worthy of me. [38] Whoever does
> not take up their cross and follow me is not
> worthy of me.

Clearly, Jesus is suggesting that allegiance to his
lordship would result in division among relationships,
even close ones. Just as Jesus had this effect on those
who encountered him, so also the Spirit of Christ
(Holy Spirit) has this same affect on people even
today. Because the Holy Spirit confronts those things
outside God's will (human tradition and personal
preferences), He is blamed for the commotion He is
said to cause. Perhaps the blame belongs to those
who oppose His lordship. Still others, believe the
emphasis on the Holy Spirit is a distraction from the
person of Jesus and his gospel mission of evangelism.
You cannot say that Jesus is jealous (in a bad way) of
the Holy Spirit receiving too much attention. Jesus
is the one who sent the Holy Spirit to continue his
ministry in the earth.

The Holy Spirit is a diversion

Sometimes the ministry of the Holy Spirit
is seen as a "bless me" diversion from some of
the more important tasks of the church, especially
evangelism. Once again, the false juxtaposition of

the Holy Spirit as a rival to evangelism is unbiblical and born out of an evangelical desire to privilege the salvation experience over the filling or sanctification experience of the Holy Spirit. First of all, it should be noted it was in the outpouring of the Holy Spirit that the greatest evangelistic results occurred in the church.[41] Secondly, as this community well knows, how can it be an unwelcome diversion or less of a priority to seek an intimate relationship with Jesus over all other concerns? It is the Holy Spirit that makes this intimate connection with Jesus possible. It is true that when believers focus on their own personal love experiences with Jesus (through the Holy Spirit), they may become myopic in regard to the mission of the kingdom. The same thing happened with Peter at the Mount of Transfiguration. However, a strong devotional experience with Jesus does not compete with the ministry of Jesus, including evangelism and other things. The problem begins when believers put their eyes on the "feel good" experiences, as if they want to use the Holy Spirit for their own purposes.[42]

---

41 In Acts 2, three thousand people were added to the church in a day because of the convicting power of the Holy Spirit.

42 I concur that the manifest presence of the Holy Spirit provides a deep and rewarding feeling when he is touching

Probably the biggest stumbling block to evangelicals is some of the odd behavior or individuals who are affected by the activities of the Holy Spirit.

Manifestations are undignified

There has been some suggestion that certain manifestations are undignified and by their very nature call attention to the person manifesting (and thus away form God), that they are potentially a distraction to important matters that are being conducted, and that the manifestations themselves are unworthy of the dignity of God. Objections to manifestations presuppose the following:

1. A person is exhibiting a need for attention, spiritual affirmation or attention. This of course presumes that the person is acting our of their own flesh apart from the actions of the Holy Spirit, or at

---

or ministering to you—as opposed to His convicting a person, or confronting a demon. However, the kingdom of God is not about these rewarding experiences, although they make the relationship rich (who doesn't want to be "loved on" by their heavenly Father?) If the Holy Spirit was a Jacuzzi, how much would be accomplished to advance the kingdom, if everyone stayed in the Jacuzzi and did not "go and make disciples?" This is the Peter syndrome at the Mount of Transfiguration—let's build tents and camp here and enjoy this experience.

least using the manifestations of the Holy Spirit as a way of gaining significance or as being accepted by a group that values manifestations. This doesn't abrogate the activities of the Holy Spirit as an expression of God's life in the church, but instead calls attention to the fact that people can pervert what God is doing to promote themselves. However, there are plenty of examples where evangelical preachers have used their preaching and administrative/people skills to promote themselves and gain a certain level of renown and significance. This is done without the reliance on the Holy Spirit. The answer is not to quench the activity of the Holy Spirit, but to teach the immature how to better relate to the Holy Spirit in an honorable way. There is the additional assumption that God would not want to cause people to act out publically under His influence, as if this is an interruption or a distraction to what He really wants to see happen (assumed by evangelicals to be the "order of service" they have planned beforehand). In 1 Corinthians 14:26, it says, "²⁶ What then shall we say, brothers and sisters? When you come together, each of you has a hymn, or a word of instruction, a revelation, a tongue or an interpretation. **Everything must be done so that the church may be built up [my emphasis].** ²⁷ If anyone speaks in a tongue, two—or at the most three—should speak, one at a time, and someone must interpret." If you look at the traditional order of worship in some churches, very little of the congregational participation is represented by this passage of scripture in the evangelical church. Notice, Paul says, "Everything must be done so that the church may be built up." First, far more people participate other than just the paid staff during a worship service. Second, tongues is also one of the things that "must be done" for the church to be built up. God is a great multi-tasker, he can do many things at the same time through the influence of His Holy Spirit. It is not chaos to Him; it is orchestration. Often times, God will actually use people to publicly demonstrate his message. Ezekiel was told by God to lie on his side for an extended period of time.[43] God made him the center of attention because Ezekiel, himself, was the message.

2. A person is manifesting a demon and

---

43 (Ezekiel 4:4-5) [4] "Then lie on your left side and put the sin of the people of Israel upon yourself. You are to bear their sin for the number of days you lie on your side. [5] I have assigned you the same number of days as the years of their sin. So for 390 days you will bear the sin of the people of Israel. [6] "After you have finished this, lie down again, this time on your right side, and bear the sin of the people of Judah. I have assigned you 40 days, a day for each year.

something "dirty" about the experience offends God, is unpleasant to the believer, or even dangerous (as in one could catch it). Demons are not an interruption to the agenda of God in a worship service or in any other activity. Jesus came (was manifested) to destroy the works of the evil one (1 John 3:8b). When a demon manifests it is being driven to the surface (losing its ability to hide in the dark) and is at the point to be cast out to the glory of God and his Christ. Jesus said, "If I cast out demons by the Spirit of God, then the Kingdom of God has come upon you." We pray in our services: "Thy Kingdom come they will be done on earth as it is in heaven" There are no demons in heaven; they are cast down, so on earth they should be cast out. They don't belong in a believer's life, and the presence of Christ and his kingdom is the power to drive them out. In fact, if demons are not fleeing, then has the kingdom of God come in your church? Sooner or later one discovers that God is not concerned with our comfort or dignity. He instead is concerned with the level of yieldedness we are willing to grant to his Spirit in order for Christ to rule in our lives. Manifestations are a way to remind believers that they are not in control. God is not a gentleman in the sense that he has to ask our permission to do anything. He is God, and he does as he pleases. He would like our consent or even more so our pursuit of His touch, but our refusal to give it does not mean he is hindered from acting if he chooses to do so. We cannot safely sit in judgment of God and his working. The real obstacle to experiencing the fullness of the Spirit the Lord has for you has to do with an unwillingness to totally yield to the Holy Spirit's advances toward you. The central obstacle to yielding to the Holy Spirit is a desire to retain a measure of control in your relationship with Him. In short, you do not fully trust the Holy Spirit enough to totally yield to him. In the next two chapters, the manifestations of the Holy Spirit will be discussed from a biblical perspective.

The BIG point: You have to learn how to trust the Holy Spirit. He is the life, power and revelation behind all that we do and all that we are. Trust the Holy Spirit as you would trust Christ. Trust the Holy Spirit as Jesus trusted the Father.

CHAPTER SEVEN: TONGUES, THE DEAL BREAKER

While most of the gifts can either be explained away or re-interpreted, the gift of tongues or the manifestations of tongues is particularly difficult for evangelicals to accept. One of the cultural difficulties to be overcome is the association of tongues with the Pentecostal denominations. Instead of viewing tongues as a biblical gift, it is seen as the preeminent marker for Pentecostals. To speak in tongues makes you Pentecostal (an abrogation of Baptist, Methodist or other denominations) instead of making you more biblical. While there are legitimate questions involving tongues from a doctrinal perspective, most evangelicals reject tongues out of hand because: 1. They have not experienced the phenomena, 2. The church they attend either teaches against tongues or does not teach on tongues as a legitimate experience at all, and 3. The reformed doctrine of the "baptism with the Holy Spirit" is subsumed in the salvation experience and this discounts the gift of tongues. In such a hostile environment toward tongues, it is likely that few evangelicals will ever see the healthy exercise of tongues in their congregations.   Does it make sense to go to an "authority" on tongues when she or he has never experienced the phenomena? There is no less bias on those who have not had the experience as it is with those who actually have experienced tongues.

Evangelicals take one of several paths to minimize the supernatural nature of tongues and their importance in the life of the church. First of all, they claim that tongues are simply a known language that the speaker has not learned, but supernaturally has been given the speaker. Thus, the Acts 2 expression of tongues is generalized to include all the other expressions of tongues mentioned in the book of Acts. However, it is clear from the other passages in Acts and Paul's treatment of tongues that a known language does not fit the context of the other passages. The Acts 10 passage concerning Cornelius records him and his household speaking in tongues as Peter preached to them. In this passage, there is no indication that the language is a known language unknown to the speaker. Furthermore, Paul in 1 Cor. 13:1 talks about the tongues of men and of angels. These angelic tongues do not correspond to any known language. In fact, Paul says in 1 Cor. 12:10 that God/Holy Spirit gives a gift of interpretation for this angelic tongue. If the tongue was a known language and uttered in a congregation then it makes sense that it was for someone who spoke that language (like in Acts 2), but this tongue has to be interpreted by a spiritual gift. Furthermore, this tongue is addressed to God himself, which makes the use of a known language a mere complication of the communication between the believer and God. Since it is the Holy Spirit that is actually praying through the believer, it makes sense that the language the Holy Spirit uses would be one that is most clearly spiritual and in tune with God.

Once it is determined that tongues is not just a known language that is unknown to the speaker, the next question raised by evangelicals is: How do we know that the tongues that are being spoken are from God and not just an expression of the demonic? It is true that demonic tongues do exist, just like demons exist (demons are angels that lost their first estate). The tongues of the Holy Spirit, however, bring a person closer to God and build the individual up. Demonic tongues do neither. Other pagan religions from the first century had ecstatic experiences and not just Christianity. During these ecstatic moments tongues sometimes was used. This provides little assurance to evangelicals who perhaps view tongues as a demonic expression. However, the way that you tell the difference between the two is to have and an intimate relationship with the Holy Spirit and to speak in a tongue that is derived from Him.

The charge that tongues was a cultural expression of pagan religions in Corinth and that they "infected" the local church is not supported by the Apostle Paul who states in 1 Corinthians 14: 1. "Do not forbid speaking in tongues"(v. 39b), 2. the believer speaks to God (v. 28b), and 3. "I thank God that I speak in tongues more than all of you" (v. 13). Clearly, Paul does not view tongues as a kind of "pagan infection" that needs to be eradicated. In fact, Paul forbids the churches from banishing tongues from their services. Since tongues is the voice of the Holy Spirit speaking praises to God (Acts 2) or the Holy Spirit uttering mysteries (revelation about what is upon God's heart- v. 2b), to forbid tongues is like telling the Holy Spirit to "shut up!" At best, this is presumption and at worse an offense to Almighty God and the Christ. Yet, how many evangelical churches have a policy of censorship that if not explicitly stated is still an "unwritten" but culturally understood norm. "If you want to do that, then another church would be a better choice." For those who pride themselves upon being "biblical" doesn't this sound somewhat relativistic? "Speak in tongues somewhere else; it is forbidden here!"

In a recent conversation with an evangelical, I was told that if churches enforced the interpretation rule (there must be an interpretation or the tongues speaker must *sit down and be quiet*), then there would be very little incidents of tongues spoken in church. This, of course, ignores the obvious, which is tongues are discouraged to begin with. Without tongues being permitted, how is it that anyone will interpret them. Furthermore, the "tongues interpretation rule" is not for the tongues speaker to sit down and be quiet. The scripture states in 1 Cor. 14:28b that the tongues speaker is to "keep silent in the church" (do not speak loud enough so that people believe s/he is addressing the congregation) and *speak to himself and to God*. So, tongues are not stopped but only redirected in terms of the audience. How would evangelicals feel if they knew that the majority of their members were very quietly speaking in tongues to themselves and God? This is not just a mental activity like silent prayer. The idea of "speaking" means saying something aloud or it is not speaking.

One of the main criticisms about tongues is that it is just gibberish because the mind is not engaged. It is true that the mind is not engaged in regard to understanding what is being said, but that does not mean there isn't an interpretation available.

However, that interpretation has to be trusted. This is sensible. When I preach in Mexico I use an interpreter (my Spanish is not that good). I have to trust that the interpreter is giving the exact meaning of my words. This is true of any unknown language to the hearer. That is why Paul states that all languages have "meaning." 1 Corinthians 14:10-14 states, "[10] Undoubtedly there are all sorts of languages in the world, yet *none of them is without meaning* [my emphasis].[11] If then I do not grasp the meaning of what someone is saying, I am a foreigner to the speaker, and the speaker is a foreigner to me.[12] So it is with you. . . .[13] For this reason the one who speaks in a tongue should pray that they may interpret what they say.[14] For if I pray in a tongue, my spirit prays, but my mind is unfruitful." One should note that Paul is comparing a person who speaks in tongues to a foreigner who speaks a different language. Both require interpreters, and, more importantly, both languages have meaning even if that meaning is not clearly known by the hearer. Paul legitimizes tongues, but affirms a public tongue is not useful to an audience unless the tongue is interpreted.

Apparently, not everyone who speaks in tongues has the same kind of experiences. For me, I did not speak in tongues when I was filled (baptized) with the Holy Spirit. I had an encounter with the Holy

Spirit during the 1980s (a move of the Holy Spirit among Baptists called the Third Wave). This move among evangelicals did not privilege speaking in tongues. While many of the leaders of the movement probably did speak in tongues, it was considered too divisive to be emphasized. During this time frame, I never heard anyone giving a public tongue in those "Spirit-filled" Baptist churches that I attended. The emphasis was on gifts of healing and deliverance (both ministries were classically confirmed in the ministry of Jesus). These evangelicals acknowledged a much broader array of gifts (manifestations of the Holy Spirit as described in 1 Corinthians 12:7-11)[44] as an indicator of one having been "filled" with the Holy Spirit. This was my experience. I began to feel the power of the Holy Spirit which led to

---

44 1 Corinthians 12:7-11 [7]Now to each one the manifestation of the Spirit is given for the common good. [8] To one there is given through the Spirit a message of wisdom, to another a message of knowledge by means of the same Spirit, [9] to another faith by the same Spirit, to another gifts of healing by that one Spirit,[10] to another miraculous powers, to another prophecy, to another distinguishing between spirits, to another speaking in different kinds of tongues, and to still another the interpretation of tongues. [11] All these are the work of one and the same Spirit, and he distributes them to each one, just as he determines.

the healing of individuals and the gift of "word of knowledge." When I spoke about my experience to Charismatics (those who had an encounter with the Holy Spirit with speaking in tongues) they told me I had not been "baptized"/ "filled" with the Holy Spirit because it did not match the biblical accounts for the experience. Imagine that--Charismatics as concerned about being biblical as much as evangelicals. Despite the fact my experience did not agree with their theology, nevertheless, I had no doubt that I had been baptized/filled with the Holy Spirit. In fact, tongues--as evidence of being baptized/filled with the Holy Spirit--is not the main agenda of God. He commands (through Paul in Ephesians 4:18) that all believers should be continuously filled with the Holy Spirit. Tongues are a by-product, along with other gifts/manifestations of the Holy Spirit. The main event is the Holy Spirit's empowering. This should be an encouragement to evangelicals who desire to move more in the things of God, but just can't get over the "tongues-thingy."

I, however, was not satisfied with the idea that I should limit God in any way in my life. I wanted everything that God had for me. That was why I asked for the gift of tongues. It happened in March of 1986. There was a ministry team from The Eagle's Nest that came to my Baptist church to support a preacher, Rick Godwin, who was leading a revival in our church. At some point during the day, I asked the team if they would pray for me so that I might receive the gift of speaking in tongues. I told them I wanted everything the Lord had for me. I did not know what to expect, but the team gathered around me and began speaking in tongues. I closed my eyes to concentrate (mentally), not realizing they simply expected me to speak without thinking. Undaunted, they continued to speak in tongues. I began to see a string of words/syllables running through my mind like a ticker tape, only much quicker. It was so fast I couldn't quite make out each word, but I tried to speak whatever word I could grasp. As I haltingly tried to speak the few words I could make out, the team said "That's it! Keep going, louder, louder." In frustration, I said, "I can't read the words, they are moving too fast!" I overheard one of the team members say to the leader, "That's not how it is supposed to work." The leader said, "He is so much into his head, God is letting him see the words." When he said that, the words in my head slowed down enough so that I could read an entire phrase. When I did that I just kept going without seeing any more words—they just began to flow out of me as I chose to speak. Interestingly enough, the experience seemed a little anti-climatic to me. Divorced from the initial coming of the power of the Holy Spirit in my earlier experience, tongues did not have the same kind of effect that others claimed for the baptism/filling of the Holy Spirit with the evidence of speaking in tongues. After about an hour, I began to question the experience, somewhat. How did I know it was the Holy Spirit speaking through me, or it was just me making up words? If I had thought about it more closely, I would have realized that I actually saw the language in my head. This was something I could not have made up. These words had no correspondence to any language I knew. However, having experienced the physical manifestation of tingling in my hands when the Holy Spirit came on me and subsequent tingling when He was doing his work, I decided I would conduct an experiment. I went by myself into the empty auditorium and began to speak in tongues; I began to feel a sense of tingling in my hands. The more I spoke in tongues the stronger the tingling sensation that ensued. I began to feel a stirring inside. I decided that the act of speaking in tongues was consistent with the manifestations and actions of the Holy Spirit I had previously experienced. Since that time, I have experienced a variety of benefits from speaking in tongues, and I have never doubted their authenticity in my life.

Some believers live their entire lives without

speaking in tongues. If tongues are that important, then why isn't the lack of tongues in the lives of believers more detrimental to their Christian experience? The answer to that question is that you don't know what you don't have; if you have never seen a microwave you would not know the the convenience or benefits it can have on your life. At this point, it is good to explain the potential benefits of speaking in tongues.

First, it should be noted that speaking in tongues is a doorway to the supernatural. Because tongues is purely a spiritual event, bypassing the mind, it "primes the pump" for supernatural experiences. Unfortunately, the mind oftentimes stands in critical evaluation (doubt) regarding spiritual experiences. The ability to speak with one's spirit in connection with the Holy Spirit opens the door to revelation/connection with God. This benefit is described by the apostle Paul in 1 Corinthians 14:2 where he sates, ² For anyone who speaks in a tongue does not speak to people but to God. Indeed, no one understands them; they *utter mysteries* [**my emphasis**] by the Spirit." Paul uses the term mysteries, in the Greek *musterion*, to speak of those things that God has hidden in the past, but now is ready to reveal. What Paul suggests is that the things that God has hidden, or revealed by the Holy Spirit through tongues, becomes available when someone is given the ability to interpret tongues. Paul said he spoke in tongues more than anyone at Corinth. We also are told that Paul had surpassing revelation that even Peter himself had difficulty in understanding. Paul spoke of the time he was in a trance and did not know whether he was in his body or out of his body and was taken to the third heaven. Clearly, it is possible that the ability to speak in tongues opened up an avenue of revelation for Paul. In essence, through the ability to interpret tongues, Paul gained a new understanding as touching the things of the Spirit and God's own heart. He confirms this when he states that the Holy Spirit knows the heart of God, even as a man's own spirit knows his own heart (1 Corinthians 2:11). Paul makes it clear that the Holy Spirit is the one who gives the believer wisdom, revelation, and the ability for believers to know the heart of God. But how is this revelation conveyed? It is conveyed either by prophecy or the interpretation of tongues. In 1 Corinthians 14:5 Paul states, "I would like every one of you to speak in tongues, but I would rather have you prophesy.[45] The one

45 Oddly enough, some Evangelicals equate prophesy simply with preaching, claiming that it is "forth-telling" primarily, rather than fore-telling. The juxtaposition of

these two terms do not do the concept of prophecy justice. Prophecy is the speaking forth of divine revelation that comes from God by way of the Holy Spirit. Sometimes the revelation is predictive, sometimes it is ethical, and sometimes it is instructional and exhortative. It functions as a quality within the evangelical notion of preaching. Let's be honest. If you listen to enough sermons you know that they are a compilation of jokes, anecdotes, vision casting, current events, opinion, cajoling, material from commentaries, quotes of famous people None of this does justice to the term prophecy (Let him who speaks let him speak the oracles of God--1 Peter 4:11-- If any man speak, let him speak as the oracles of God; if any man minister, let him do it as of the ability which God giveth: that God in all things may be glorified through Jesus Christ, to whom be praise and dominion forever and ever. Amen. KJV). Furthermore, preaching doesn't describe the ministry of Agabus, who predicted a famine and Paul's imprisonment. However, if you are fortunate, a Holy Spirit directed interpretation/ explanation and application of the scripture will feed your soul and may be seen as having some degree of prophetic character. I am a teacher/ preacher or a preacher who teaches under the direction of the Holy Spirit in my delivery. I know the difference between prophetic/Holy Spirit led teaching/preaching and the homiletical/rhetorical gimmics and structures of sermons I have heard. Clearly, this footnote is a rabbit trail from the above discussion (which is why it is a footnote), but it is important to point out if you want to change the core definition of prophecy to claim it is simply preaching, who prophesies is greater than the one who speaks in tongues, unless someone interprets, so that the church may be edified." Prophecy is greater UNLESS tongues are interpreted, then tongues is on a par with prophecy. Prophecy is not simply preaching as some evangelicals would lead us to believe because the correspondence between tongues being useful and prophecy is that prophecy is revelation in an understood language. Both have to do with revelation; preaching has to do with preparation and delivery of the scripture as it applies to people's lives. There are things that humans cannot know unless the Holy Spirit reveals it to them. Today, evangelicals know what God SAID through the scriptures as the apostles HEARD the voice of God and then recorded what he said. While, hearing the voice of God today cannot result in the once for all delivered WORD OF GOD, believer's can still hear "a word" from God as direction involving specific circumstances. There will never be any additional material added to our bible, the scriptures. However, if we value the scriptures we must understand that revelation comes through the Holy Spirit, and that is what makes Christianity different from a lot of other religions. As Paul states

---

then how trustworthy is the treatment of other concepts considered more controversial.

in 1 Corinthians 2: 6-16:

> [6] We do, however, speak a message of wisdom among the mature, but not the wisdom of this age or of the rulers of this age, who are coming to nothing. [7] No, *we declare God's wisdom, a mystery that has been hidden* [my emphasis] and that God destined for our glory before time began. [8] None of the rulers of this age understood it, for if they had, they would not have crucified the Lord of glory. [9] However, as it is written:
>
>> "What no eye has seen,
>> what no ear has heard,
>> and what no human mind has conceived"—
>> the things God has prepared for those who love him—
>
> [10] *these are the things God has revealed to us by his Spirit.* [my emphasis; the things that are reveled are those things that the human mind could not conceive of]. The Spirit searches all things, even the deep things of God. [11] For who knows a person's thoughts except their own spirit within them? In the same *way no one knows the*

thoughts of God except the Spirit of God. [my emphasis] [12] What we have received is not the spirit of the world, but the Spirit who is from God, *so that we may understand*[my emphasis]what God has freely given us. [13] This is what we speak, not in words taught us by human wisdom but *in words taught by the Spirit, explaining spiritual realities with Spirit-taught words*[my emphasis]. [14] The person without the Spirit does not accept the things that come from the Spirit of God but considers them foolishness, and *cannot understand them because they are discerned only through the Spirit* [my emphasis]. [15] The person with the Spirit makes judgments about all things, but such a person is not subject to merely human judgments,[16] for,"Who has known the mind of the Lord so as to instruct him? But we have the mind of Christ.

Other benefits to speaking in tongues includes: 1. The building up edification of the believer. (1 Corinthians 14:18-19)(cp with Jude 20); 2. With tongues the Holy Spirit intercedes for us with groaning, i.e., praying according to the will of God apart from the limitations of human language; and 3. The revealing of hidden mystery to the one who interprets the tongue (1 Cor. 14:2).[46]

     I am not afraid to examine the best argument of evangelicals in regard to speaking in tongues. John P. Newport, (now deceased) Professor of Philosophy of Religion at Southwestern Baptist Theological Seminary (my alma mater) wrote an in depth article called "Speaking With Tongues." I received it from another Baptist preacher years ago along with his notes. As best as I can remember, it was given to me in the late 1980s, probably with the desire to save me from some gross error. I re-discovered the article even as I began writing this book. Dr. Newport was a well-respected evangelical professor, and his article is generally well-reasoned and reasonable. However, after having done additional doctoral work in the field of rhetoric, I recognize certain "tells" or subtle demeaning terms and constructs to dissuade, in this case Baptists, believers from speaking with tongues. It is not my goal to speak in any way that diminishes the *ethos* of Dr. Newport. Instead, my goal is to point out that what purports to be a fair examination of tongues can have an underlying tone that breeds disrespect.

---

46 2 For anyone who speaks in a tongue[a] does not speak to people but to God. Indeed, no one understands them; they utter mysteries by the Spirit.

For example, let's begin with the use of certain terms (capitalized) that I will quote in context. "The Eastern Orthodox churches ALLOWED this gift under control, through the ages [allowed is different than supported]. The book of Acts is a basic source for the doctrine of the SO-CALLED third aspect of the Spirit's work [so-called is used to express one's clear opposition to the concept]. Previously, Newport implies there was no Christian tradition beyond justification and sanctification for centuries implying "being filled by the Spirit" is a recent (thus suspect) addition to the theology of the church. Tell it to Paul who lived in the first century. By the way, Dispensationalism is a recent eschatological (end-times) position dating in the 1800s. What about that? In reference to Paul addressing the Corinthian church regarding tongues, Newport admits that tongues should not be forbidden, but that Paul said they must be STRICTLY CONTROLLED. Paul does not use that "tone" in his letter to the church at Corinth. The Corinthian church had fallen into the imbalanced idea that if tongues were God's language then they were supposed to spend the entire service with everyone speaking in tongues. Paul wisely corrects this practice (not doctrine) with his own SUGGESTION as to what is better for the church. He was responding to a PROBLEM in the church, not creating a doctrine.

107

Tongues, the Deal Breaker

I have <u>never</u> been in a Charismatic church where they <u>only</u> spoke in tongues or did so to the exclusion of other ministries. *If the problem ever does arise then this particular application of scripture to this specific problem should be exercised.* In other words, Paul's ADVICE (albeit inspired by the Spirit) is CULTURALLY SPECIFIC. Paul had to address women flaunting their freedom in the church (a kind of excess or abuse) and tells them their constant questions and interruption of the services needed to stop. They were to ask their husbands their questions at home. He says, "Women should remain silent in the church." So, Paul wants them STRICTLY CONTROLLED? Most Bible scholars view this passage as dealing with a specific culturally determined issue, and it is not as applicable to our churches today. Here's one. Paul says you should not get drunk at the Lord's Supper. Well, Paul, thanks for that bit of inspiration. No duh! Don't get me wrong. What he says is led by the Spirit to prohibit debauchery and division in the church. However, it doesn't need to be turned into a policy and hung on the wall of a church or put into the bulletin. Paul gave divinely inspired specific advice to a church that had a specific problem. So let me ask the evangelical church this question: How likely is it that tongues are going to get out of hand in your services? Not likely, is it. Then why use this specific

advice of scripture to hammer other Christians about
something that doesn't occur in your church (do you
want them to hammer you for forbidding tongues?)?
If IT HAPPENS in your church, instead of being afraid,
you should be confident that there is a loving way to
apply scripture to support your bias against tongues.
State your biblical policy; don't become angry and
escort the person out of your church as if they came
to church drunk-"they are not drunk as you suppose."
Acting reasonably is a godly trait and is an aspect of
"Heavenly Wisdom" (James 3:16-18).[47] Moving on.

Newport suggests that "a constant EFFORT to
WORK UP to a "FREE-WHEELING" ecstatic experience
can be habit-forming [like only listening to sermons
but not putting any of them into practice-Hebrews
5:11-14 and James 1:22-24[48]] and become an end in

---

47 [16] For where you have envy and selfish ambition, there
you find disorder and every evil practice. [17] But the
wisdom that comes from heaven is first of all pure; then
peace-loving, considerate, submissive, full of mercy and
good fruit, impartial and sincere. [18] Peacemakers who sow
in peace reap a harvest of righteousness (my emphasis).

48 [22] Do not merely listen to the word, and so deceive
yourselves. Do what it says. [23] Anyone who listens to the
word but does not do what it says is like someone who looks
at his face in a mirror [24] and, after looking at himself, goes
away and immediately forgets what he looks like.

itself. Newport is suggesting that tongues is a part of "ecstatic" experience that is derived from human effort apart from the activity of the Holy Spirit (effort to work up) and is not controlled by the Holy Spirit (free-wheeling) and is similar to a drug or a bad habit (implied). Taken together in connection to what an ecstatic experience means, Newport, apparently, does not understand the concept as it applies to the Christian church. He goes on to say, "These SELF-CENTERED experiences [unlike preachers or evangelists who win people to Jesus only so they can have notoriety, bigger ministries and more money] can be used to bypass the struggles which are a part of Christian growth." Hmmm . . . so I guess he is suggesting, in connection to the idea of habit forming, ecstatic experiences in general and tongues in particular are like an escape mechanism (drug or alcohol) that prevents a person from facing his or her problems. So connecting with Jesus is a bad idea when you are facing problems, so what you should do is just "grunt" through your problems stoically (man-up)?

     This is part of a theme that is carried through the article--tongues are a crutch for weak, immature people (oh my, there is no pride associated with that position given the fact evangelicals don't NEED the experience). Wait a minute! The crutch and weak

110

people argument is used by unbelievers against Christians (evangelicals) because of their NEED for Jesus! Drawing from the article we read: "Speaking in tongues EVIDENTLY gave him [the apostle Paul] a real outlet for PENT-UP FEELINGS which he could not express in words (Romans 8:26)." Poor emotionally stressed Paul needed tongues to make himself FEEL better. Really? Paul says we do not always know "what to pray for." Romans 8:26-27 states, "Likewise the Spirit helps us in our weakness [of understanding, not emotional disturbance]. For we <u>do not know</u> what to pray for as we ought [this is a matter of revelation, not a release of emotion], but the Spirit himself intercedes for us with groanings too deep for words." In fairness, Newport probably focuses on "groanings" to suggest a release of emotion, but the emphasis is not on us but the work of the Holy Spirit in utterances (tongues that sound like groaning) interceding for us. The point is some prayers cannot be made using human language—the matter is too deep, too complicated. Who is doing the groaning? Newport suggests it is the person, but the actor in the event is the Spirit who is praying. The safe answer is that the Holy Spirit, who knows our hearts and is intimately connected to the heart of the Father, speaks for us through our unintelligible speech/utterances that sound like groaning.[49]

In an effort to minimize the role of tongues in a believer's life, Newport uses several additional rhetorical moves. First, he suggests it is not a <u>central</u> DOCTRINE. I would agree with him in at least two ways: 1. It is a practice that is done more than a tenet to be believed in; and 2. Tongues does not connect with any core-essential doctrine regarding salvation, although it does connect with the person of the Holy Spirit. Yet, once again, there are beliefs held by evangelicals that are considered important but are not essential/central doctrines, mostly because they have to do with PRACTICE. Both baptism and the Lord's Supper are celebrated differently in Protestant churches. The role of women in leadership positions in the church can vary. Church government, methods of giving, how one is granted membership in a local church body, and so forth, are not central doctrines

---

49 When my wife was seriously injured with a brain trauma and in a coma, I was in the waiting room of the hospital in prayer for her. I remember speaking in tongues, but it was different from any previous experience I had had up to that point. The tongue was staccato and I sensed a deep moving of the Holy Spirit combined with an anguish in my heart. At that moment it came to me that the tongue I was speaking was the groaning Paul was talking about in Romans 8.

of the church even if they are matters that tend to define and divide one denomination from the other. In short, tongues is an additional legitimate expression of the Holy Spirit beyond the essential role of conversion/justification. The later work of the Spirit all believer's hold in common, hence, essential/ central. So what is the difference if I say tongues is not central as opposed to Newport saying the same thing? I don't have a bias against the practice, as we shall see as further statements made by him are discussed.

Newport goes on to say: "Paul states that the gift of tongues is an INFERIOR or LOWER gift." Paul never uses those exact words; this is Newport's interpretation and it has a "tone" to it. Paul says, in 1 Corinthians 14:1, tongues rise to the level of prophecy when they are interpreted (which should always be done when addressing a congregation). Paul maintains that believers should "earnestly desire the spiritual gifts [that includes tongues and the interpretation of tongues], especially that [they] may prophesy." Now if prophesy is preaching, as some evangelicals maintain, then when tongues that address the congregation are interpreted it is the same as preaching to the congregation. Let's face it. Preaching is held in high regard by evangelicals, so logically, when public tongues is interpreted in a church that permits this earnestly desired gift, they should support tongues that are biblically administered in their churches. Additionally, the ranking of the gifts, in which tongues and its interpretation comes last in the list (1 Cor. 12:7-10), does not suggest that Paul intended a ranking in order of importance, as Newport suggests. In fact, later in chapter 12, verse 28 of 1 Corinthians, Paul states, "And God has appointed in the church first apostles, second prophets, third teachers, then miracles, then gifts of healing, helping [service which is the most commonly used gift in the church, yet it is ranked after miracles and healing], administrating [the task that takes up most pastor's time], and *various kinds of tongues* [my emphasis]." This list implies a ranking, but scholars cannot conclude if it is a ranking of importance. It might by a ranking of which came first in the church. There are some noteworthy matters to be considered in this passage. The most "necessary" gifts for the ongoing functioning in the church appear midway in the list—serving (followers) and administrators (leaders). Miracles and healings, which are not plentiful in most churches, rank above those two gifts. Furthermore, there are various kinds of tongues (at least two, but more than that implied). This is important regarding what Paul says next. He goes on to say in verse 29 through 31, "Are all

Apostles? Are all prophets? [note: these are offices, because later Paul says all believers should pursue the spiritual gift of prophecy] Are all teachers? Do all work miracles? [Jesus said anyone who believed in him could-John 14:11-12]. Do all possess gifts of healing? [yet, Jesus commanded his followers to heal the sick]. The implied answer in the Greek is no. Paul is saying there are specific ministry gifted individuals who exercise these abilities on a regular basis, while believers in general, may exercise aspects of these abilities as moved by the Holy Spirit.

How serious is the Holy Spirit regarding the expression of tongues in public services? Perhaps a cautionary tale is warranted at this point. After the Holy Spirit showed up at the Baptist church where I was a pastor, we agreed that we would retain our denominational affiliation and permit personal ministry (healing etc) through the ministry of prayer and the laying on of hands, and if anyone publicly spoke in tongues it would have to be interpreted. Under these guidelines we progressed as a "spirit-filled" Baptist church for a number of years, until a woman publicly spoke in tongues, and then it was interpreted. At the next business meeting (Baptists believe that a 51% majority decides the will of God in most matters, as they have congregational rule) a group of members came together to pass a motion to ban the speaking in tongues in our public services. I pleaded with them not to do so; they had the number of votes to succeed in their task. I told them they were violating the scripture and the covenant we had been operating under for years. They would not be dissuaded, and so tongues were officially banned from our public worship services. This was a Wednesday night, and, come Sunday morning, the tangible presence of the Holy Spirit, was not discernible in the services—the services seemed dead, lifeless. There was a man named Rodgers in the church that I knew regularly heard from God (Rodgers was not present on Wednesday night, nor did he know what had happened), so as he was leaving the church, I asked him if he noticed anything different about the services. He said, "It was dead this morning. I didn't sense the Holy Spirit at all." I replied, "Did you ask God what the problem was?" He said, "I did. The Lord told me, 'those people have offended me.' Do you know what He was talking about?" I then explained to Rogers what happened Wednesday night. He said, "That will do it." That evening in the Sunday night service the Holy Spirit showed up, and I felt His tangible presence and ministry. I looked out over the congregation and noticed that none of the members who voted to ban tongues was present in the services. As if to emphasize the importance of their actions, there was a member who had been out of town during the Wednesday night meeting, but if he had been there he would have voted with them. I was interested in finding out what Rodgers would say, so after services, I posed the same question I had asked that morning. "Rogers did you notice anything different about the services tonight?" He said, "The Holy Spirit was in our services tonight." I asked him, "Did you ask the Lord about it." He said, "Yes." He said the Lord told him, "None of my antagonists are here tonight." I told him he was correct. He did not know who was at the Wednesday meeting, so I knew he had heard from God about the matter. Over the next couple of months the grace had lifted off the church, and relationships were strained among the members. In short, the life had gone out of the church (You have to have been exposed to the presence of the Holy Spirit in a tangible way in order to know when He is no longer tangibly present. It makes one think about how many congregations are not certain if the Holy Spirit is actually present and working in their midst). From the moment the decision had been made to ban tongues, I decided not to make it a divisive issue. I continued to do ministry sessions under the power of the Holy Spirit in some of the side rooms during the week with certain members who were

117

open to the Holy Spirit, but the Holy Spirit stayed away from the services. However, after a few months traditionalist members of the congregation started coming to me, asking me what was wrong with the church. Although they were not "Spirit-filled," even they knew something was wrong. I told them that I did not intend to bring this subject up again, but if they wanted to reverse what they were experiencing they needed to rescind the motion that banned the speaking of tongues in public services. They did just that, and the Holy Spirit came back into our services.

Now then, what is the point? The point is simply this: you can offend or grieve the Holy Spirit by forbidding Him from expressing his voice in the church. Furthermore, if you are able to sense his tangible presence, then you will be able to tell when the Holy Spirit withholds himself. If not, you may never know what you are missing. On the other hand, if tongues never happen in the church, then it is less likely actions will be taken to offend Him. Yet, the question remains: Are there other ways in which believers and churches have offended or grieved the Holy Spirit?

Because I have the ability to tangibly or physically experience the presence of God (it is a tingling sensation that is located mostly on my hands), I know when something occurs in a worship service that is more welcomed or less welcomed by the Holy Spirit. I remember one occasion that the Holy Spirit was growing in power during our worship service, and the people were noticeably being touched. The worship leader decided to stick with the program and go to the next song on his agenda. I immediately felt the Holy Spirit lift off the services. I stopped him and asked him to go back to the previous song, telling him I felt the Holy Spirit wanted us to remain there. When he went back to the previous song, the Holy Spirit began to minister to the people once again.[50] If the Holy Spirit cares that much to teach us he has priorities or preferences in our worship services, then you can imagine his interest and concern regarding even more basic doctrinal matters, values, and priorities in ministry.

---

50 The problem here is obvious; you have to have someone who can discern the presence of the Lord in an objective way to notice the difference in the Spirit's activity during a worship service. I use the term objective even though it is subjectively experienced by a person because it is not a phenomena that can be created subjectively by the person.

CHAPTER EIGHT: THE ROLE OF MANIFESTATIONS

As previously stated, manifestations are a natural part of the moving/activity of the Holy Spirit. A lack of familiarity with manifestations should not be construed as a basis for an out-of-hand opposition to these same manifestations. One of the mechanisms of protection that evangelicals use to insulate themselves from manifestations of the Holy Spirit is the use of scripture to shield them from these experiences (see the chapter on the primacy of the scripture and experiences). However, an examination of the scriptures and a history of revival experiences show that manifestations of the Holy Spirit are indeed both biblical and a regular feature of revival movements throughout the history of the church.

The first question to be generally addressed is: Are the manifestations seen in Charismatic type churches biblical? While it is possible that every potential experience or manifestation may not be completely covered by a scripture, it is appropriate, if not wise, to search the scriptures to gain an

120

understanding about the nature of the experiences you encounter or experience.[51] There are those who would limit the legitimacy of a spiritual experience solely on the basis of whether or not the experience can be located or posited in the scripture. However, as the scripture itself declares, not every spiritual reality is addressed or even described in scripture. Some experiences are indeed extra-biblical (a term that makes evangelicals uncomfortable because of a reaction to Catholic affirmation of the role of tradition and extra-biblical texts as a basis for formulating doctrine) and must be judged on a wider apprehension of scripture, i.e., is Jesus glorified, does the experience result in a person living a more Christ-like life, etc. Some manifestations are indeed biblical, but they may be supported in scripture more by implication that by direct description. One reason that manifestations may not be as directly addressed in scripture is because they were either too common to warrant extended treatment in Jesus' day or they were seen as tangential to the importance of recognizing the specific result of the ministry of

---

51 When the apostle Paul first went to the Greek city of Berea, the book of Acts says that the Bereans were more noble than the other Jews Paul had encountered in Greece because they "'searched the Scriptures daily to see if what Paul was saying was true" (17.11).

121

the Holy Spirit, which is healing, deliverance and salvation. Those who are comfortable with the manifestations of the Spirit would agree with this last assessment that the result of the Holy Spirit's ministry is more important than the evidence that the Holy Spirit is ministering.

It should be noted that there is a place of questioning that is a medial position between full acceptance and rejection of manifestations as an activity of the Holy Spirit. Those who are uncertain about the place of manifestations often begin with a skeptical position. Skepticism with a desire to know the truth is different than a skepticism that is a manifestation of a position of rejection. To reserve judgment about a matter is not the same as having fully decided about a matter. In most cases, an examination of scripture and an opening of the heart to God's instruction are necessary in order to fully understand, if not embrace, the working of the Holy Spirit inclusive of the manifestations He brings.

A search of the scriptures reveals that manifestations are not considered to be central to the formulation of theological doctrine or even ethical admonition (the exception seems to be the emphasis on speaking in tongues which is a manifestation of the Holy Spirit more commonly referred to and is a doctrine of Pentecostal churches and some charismatic churches). The tendency to assign equal value to every passage of scripture regardless of its place in the genre of scripture or its subject matter is a mistake made by those who are vehement about the infallibility of the scripture. The infallibility of the scripture and the usefulness of particular scriptures in formulating doctrine are separate issues. One's belief about the atoning death of Jesus on the cross has a higher level of spiritual importance than whether or not one has a precise belief about the nature of the Holy Spirit's activity when people fall down under the "power of the Holy Spirit." That doesn't mean the later is not important, but it does mean that the spiritual consequences of unbelief regarding the atoning work of Christ on the cross has repercussions more significant than doubting the veracity of a particular manifestation of the Holy Spirit. Embracing the manifestations of the Holy Spirit may cost a person their circle of associations, but embracing a deficient view of the atonement of Christ at best could be heresy and worse a matter of jeopardizing one's spiritual condition. My point is simply this: Chill on expressions of interaction with God that have nothing to do with core doctrines of theology that affect the very salvation or welfare of the believer. This is not to say I wish to minimize the importance of the working of the Holy Spirit in the believer's life as evidenced by manifestations. The working of the Holy Spirit is essential for living the Christian life that God approves, and opposing manifestations to the extent that believer's are discouraged from experiencing the life of the Holy Spirit is unwise according to the counsel of scripture.[52] My purpose is to suggest that reactions to the manifestations of the Holy Spirit should be placed within a context that minimizes over-reaction or a knee jerk predisposition that opposes the important work of the Holy Spirit because some of the evidences of his working does not fit in with a person's predisposition or views.

Having expressed the preceding ground rules for addressing the manifestations of the Holy Spirit, a good place to begin is with the scriptural texts that touch upon some of those manifestations. At this point, the phenomena of speaking in tongues will not be addressed because it was covered in the previous chapter.

Types of Manifestations

I shall begin with the most acceptable manifestations of the Holy Spirit in regard to evangelical predilections. Godly sorrow that

---

52 "Do not put out the Spirit's fire." (1 Thessalonians 5:19 or "Do not quench the Spirit").

comes from conviction by the Holy Spirit that leads to weeping is an activity of the Holy Spirit. This manifestation is experienced internally in the emotions and the outward expression is crying. It is quite acceptable to evangelicals because it seems normal and is easily explained. In fact, most manifestations of the Holy Spirit associated with salvation are deemed acceptable because evangelicals have experienced this particular work of the Holy Spirit. You will notice that the faith one has is connected with the experiences one has. You know something is true, or real deep down, when it is realized within yourself. That is why a person with an experience is never at the mercy of someone with an argument. While this seems relativistic or subjective, all spiritual experience, for it to be valid/ real in a person's life, must be intrinsically satisfying; it must be meaningful to the individual who professes adherence to a religion or spiritual system.[53] If

---

53 The fact that there are false religions or non-Christian religions whose adherence to their religion brings them satisfaction does not abrogate this need of human existence. It simply means the TRUTH of a religious system is not based on personal satisfaction or meaningfulness. Personal satisfaction or meaningfulness reinforces the truth and increases the passion and faith of the adherent. There are some satisfactions that come

something is not subjectively experienced, it does not mean that it is objectively untrue.[54] People who have not experienced the saving knowledge of the Lord Jesus Christ do not invalidate the truth regarding Jesus as the savior through His atoning work on the cross. The same can be said for any experience that comes from the activity of the Holy Spirit. To say that it is not true or real because you

---

from belonging, altruism, family pride, nationalism, recognition, significance of place and other matters that are chiefly sociological or psychological and have nothing to do with the direct benefits of what the religion itself promises.

54 I found out, the hard way, that Texas has a law that forbids you to drive in the fast lane unless you are passing someone. What I called a "fast" lane, they call a "passing" lane. I was ignorant about the law and subjectively never experienced a ticket. Both of those things changed. As I was handed the ticket, I was told ignorance of the law is no excuse. I knew about most traffic laws. I was only ignorant about one law because the reality of that law never came upon me. Some evangelicals know the Holy Spirit and about his Life and work, but that does not mean they know everything about the Life and work of the Holy Spirit. Who does? Pentecostals and Charismatics should avoid spiritual pride, for the sake of unity, and evangelicals should stop judging and despising their brothers and sisters, for the sake of unity.

have not experienced it, while there are millions who have experienced it, is a kind of relativism based on subjectivity that is abhorred by those who hold to the concept of objective truth. God is real even though atheists deny it. Jesus is truly God and savior though other religions and cults deny it. The Holy Spirit still performs miracles, healings, and deliverance and expresses himself through all the gifts though certain Christians deny it. For me, when I accepted Christ as savior, I experienced a sense of peace and a relief as if a burden was lifted off my shoulders. I lost a fear of death, and within days I experienced a greater sense of love for my friends and concern for their spiritual condition. These manifestations of the Holy Spirit would be applauded by most evangelicals, although they may not be experienced by everyone at the moment of salvation. In fact, earlier follow-up methods of leading people to Christ (especially those used by Campus Crusade for Christ) seek to minimize the emotions. Having been trained in the use of "The Four Spiritual Laws" pamphlet, I would tell those who prayed to receive Jesus that they were to do so by faith, and it was not necessary to "feel" anything, just simply believe. While this advice was helpful in helping those whose experience was "uneventful," it ignored the obvious: a person should be different in some way after they have committed his or her life to Jesus. These con[a]firming experiences is what Paul refers to in Rom.8:16, when he states, "the Spirit bears witness with our spirit that we are the children of God."

Over time, as an evangelical, I could sense the "presence" of God in my heart and times of comfort in difficult situations. Perhaps the most supernatural experience I had prior to my baptism with the Holy Spirit was when my father had experienced a heart attack in the hospital. I was seated in the waiting room with my fiancée. She was holding my right hand while my left arm was resting on the arm of the chair. While my eyes were closed (I don't remember if we were praying) I felt someone squeezing my left hand. It was so real that I opened my eyes and looked only to find no one was there. I came to understand that the phenomenon I experienced was an angel sent to comfort me. What makes this experience different from most acceptable manifestations is the event occurred in the physical realm, outside my own body. These kinds of experiences are "super"-natural and less easily accepted. There are a number of emotions that the Holy Spirit can touch, but these are different from experiencing the emotions OF the Holy Spirit. The Holy Spirit can touch OUR emotions or He can reveal HIS emotions through us. The Holy Spirit is a person; it should not be odd to realize that

He has emotions and He expresses them. When the Holy Spirit expresses his emotions, they usually come suddenly in a way that seems strong and sometimes not connected to the thoughts that would normally occur prior to the expression of human emotions. One of the spiritual endowments I have received from the Holy Spirit is the ability to feel the emotions of God. I have met others who more or less have this ability as well. I have experienced a range of emotions expressed through the Holy Spirit. I have experienced Joy or laughter. For me, it begins with a sensation in my abdomen and a light-heartedness that leads to laughter.

I prayed for a man who was withdrawn because of a heaviness or depression. At first, I did not notice anything and went about other matters. Within a few minutes we heard riotous laughter coming from the kitchen (we were in a house church setting). He was trying to get a drink from the facet, but he kept stumbling around and even fell down as if he were drunk. At this point it is good to note that joy is the emotion of the Holy Spirit, laughter is one of the human reactions to that joy (John 17:13– having the full measure of Christ's joy).

I was in the hospital awaiting surgery when a nurse with an interesting pewter necklace came in to take my vitals. I inquired about the necklace, and

129

she said it was to the "goddess." I realized she was a Wiccan and began to witness to her about God/Jesus' elevation of women in the Middle Eastern culture. I, also, told her about a Wiccan friend I knew in college. All of a sudden, I felt the love and compassion of God come over me, and I took her hand (she was getting ready to leave after having taken my pulse) and looked her directly in the eyes and told her: "You need to know Jesus loves you very much." She slowly left the room and I didn't see her for four hours even though she was my charge nurse. I was afraid I had offended her because she was gone so long, and others had come in her place. So, I specifically asked one of the nurses to ask her to come to me. When she arrived I asked her if I had offended her and told her I did not mean to do so. She replied that was not the case and told me that she had just asked that morning if there was something more to life than what she was experiencing because she was so dissatisfied. She said that she had to go away by herself for a while to think about what I had said to her. I know that it wasn't just the words because when we locked eyes I felt the love of God pouring out of me towards her. It was the Spirit's emotion of compassion/love that impacted her (Matt. 9:36)–"When he saw the crowds, he [Jesus] was moved with compassion. . ." (Matt. 23:37) cp.–"O Jerusalem. . ."). I know this was an emotion of the Holy Spirit because I did not know her well enough to be that overcome with concern for her soul.

I was at a conference in 1990 in Kansas City listening to Jim Goll speak about intercessory burdens. He asked the Holy Spirit to show us what was on God's heart. As he mentioned several things abortion, the state of the church and the nations who did not have a strong Christian witness, I started weeping and felt a burden come on my shoulders. While these are issues that some can become emotional about, they were not matters that I had pondered during this time frame (weeping/grief: (John 11:35)–Jesus grieved in his spirit...). On another occasion I was speaking in a church that was desperately in need of revival because of their worldliness and coolness to the Holy Spirit. I was using a Ken doll to illustrate the problem of idols. I said some people think God no longer acts in the world today (I pulled off his arms), does not walk in fellowship with us like Jesus did with his disciples or God with Adam in the cool of the day (I pulled off the dolls legs. I then said: for some, God no longer speaks to us directly (I pulled off the doll's head) and held up the torso. Each time people began to laugh more and more as I dismembered the doll. I took the torso (before putting it in an elongated box) and told them, this is all that is left-- a heart of love for you and even then you are closed off to that. I put the torso in the box and laid it down. Then I realized something: 'Oh look, that box looks like a coffin.' They didn't get it, some still laughed and I felt righteous indignation/anger rising (John 2:17)–Zeal for your house has consumed me [clears the temple—it looks like anger]. However, we are taught that ministers do not get angry, so I fought the emotion as if it was trying to take over me. I told them that was the sermon, and they were to go home and think about it. I just needed them to leave because I was not comfortable with God's anger towards idolatry coming through me.

There is one emotion that I call dread that some people call the "fear of the Lord." This is not an emotion of the Holy Spirit, but instead it is the human emotion of responding to the realization of God's complete Sovereignty over one's life, i.e., He is in control of heartbeat and breathing. The problem is that the "fear of the Lord" simply means respect to some people; it is an attitude and not an emotion. This dread came on me on two occasions that are the most memorable. The first time I felt dread is when I was facing the decision of whether or not I should take a stand before my congregation having just received the baptism with the Holy Spirit. God asked me if I was ashamed of the experience and I told him no. He then asked me if I were afraid of the people and I told him yes (I was afraid and you don't want to lie to a God who already knows the true answer). God said: "You mean to tell me that you are more afraid of them than you are of me." This is when I began to experience dread or the fear of the Lord. Then He said, "If you don't take a stand for me now, it will affect your ministry for the rest of your life." For me, that choice was easy to make because my plan was to be in ministry for the rest of my life. The words from God are in quotes because they are exactly what He said. One doesn't forget such a direct speaking and dreadful experience like that –(Heb. 10:31)–"It is a fearful thing to fall into the hands of the Living God". The other time I experienced dread was when I was preaching and at the end of my sermon I was talking about the cataclysmic second coming of the Lord Jesus Christ. I began by saying he is like a bridegroom who steps out of his tent and the universe bows in humility.   The vision of his return, under the unction of the Holy Spirit, was as terrifying as encountering an angel in the scripture. I found myself engaged in a scream that crescendoed and ended with my congregation on their faces on the floor under the "fear of the Lord."

Finally, we are told in Galatians 5:22-23 that the evidence of the Holy Spirit in us is the "fruit" of the Holy Spirit. In the past, I had always assumed that it was the Spirit simply acting on our emotions, but now, there seems to be an enablement or grace that is in combination with our own emotions. It is not just human love, joy or peace, but it is a work of the Holy Spirit displaying his emotions in us, somehow embedded in our own emotions.

Specific Manifestations

Falling

One of the most common manifestations of the Spirit is the phenomena of falling, sometimes referred to as "resting in the Spirit" or in the parlance of older Pentecostal terminology as being "slain in the Spirit." The later reference is to the guards at the tomb of Jesus who fell down as if they were dead when they encountered an angel. The preferable phrase is "resting in the Spirit" in that death is really not a representative term of the experience and has a fairly negative association. People who "fall out" in the power of the Holy Spirit and find themselves "resting in the Spirit" are usually conscious. They may look around and interact with others even as they commune with the Lord. Sometimes, they are unable to move in general or unable to move only certain parts of their bodies. Under certain circumstances, God is actually ministering to the person in his sovereign power. His desire

134

is to "operate" on the individual while they are experiencing a type of divine anesthesia. In more rare cases, those who rest in the Holy Spirit may be less in touch with their surroundings, appearing even drunk (out of it) or even in a form of trance. The result of experiencing the phenomena of "resting in the spirit" is a greater appreciation of Jesus and a deeper walk with the Lord. Some scriptures that address these phenomena are as follows:

In Gen. 15:12, we read ". . . Aram fell into a deep sleep and a thick, dreadful darkness came over him." The Hebrew word *radam* literally reads, "a deep sleep fell on Abram." This is the same word that is used when God put Adam to sleep when he made Eve (Gen. 2:21; cf. 17:17: Abraham fell face down"). In 1 Sam. 19, it says, "He [Saul] stripped off his garments, and he too prophesied in Samuel's presence. He lay naked all that day and all that night. This is why people say, "Is Saul also among the prophets?" This text indicates that Saul laid on the ground for an extended period of time, perhaps up to 24 hours. *Saul lay in a prone position with God speaking through him.* This is why the prophetic troop said, "Is Saul also among the prophets?" Later, when Solomon dedicated the temple in 2 Chronicles 5:13-14, we read, "all of a sudden the temple of the Lord was filled with a cloud, and the priests could not perform their service because of the cloud, for the glory of the Lord filled the temple of God." The inability of the priests to perform their service in the temple poses a question: In what way were they hindered? Some suggest, obliquely, that the priests "fell out under the power of the Spirit" even though the text never says that the priests fell. At least the indication seems to be that under God's glory they were essentially immobilized, physically unable to perform their duties. The Hebrew word for glory, *kabod* means "a weight" and may explain why people are immobilized or drop to the floor. The phenomena of falling in God's presence might be understood as one being overcome by the weight of God. The prophet Ezekiel on a number of occasions "fell" face down when encountering the glory of the Lord (Ezek. 1:28; Ezek.3:23). Daniel when encountering the Lord also experienced this phenomenon where he was terrified and fell on [his] face (Dan. 8:17).[55] In another instance of encountering an angelic being, Daniel says, 'When I heard the sound of his words I then was lying stunned (*radam*) on the ground and

---

55 As an evangelical, I naturally assumed that he voluntarily lie prone in respect of the supernatural occurrence. However, it is not so clear how he ends up on the ground. Whatever position that is taken is an interpretation that is read into the text.

my face was toward the ground" (Dan. 10:9).

The New Testament records instances where falling down occurred upon encountering angels and even the risen Lord himself. In Mt. 17:6 it states, "When the disciples heard this, they fell face down to the ground terrified. But Jesus came and touched them. "Get up,' he said 'Don't be afraid." In Mt. 28:4, "The guards were so afraid of him [the angel] that they shook and became like dead men." People who encountered Jesus in an effort to oppose him sometimes were given a taste of the power of Jesus in his physical form. One such incident was when Judas and the soldiers came to arrest Jesus. When Jesus said,"I am he," they fell back to the ground. This response is curious because it was their purpose to apprehend Jesus. They had sufficient numbers to arrest him, and they did not seem to be afraid of Jesus at other times when he ministered. One could conclude that when Jesus said "I am he" the invocation of the phrase "I am" was an expression of God's name to Moses. The falling back/down may be seen as the imposition of God's power to demonstrate that Jesus was going to give his life willingly to be sacrificed.

The Apostle Paul "fell to the ground and heard a voice from heaven" (Acts 9.22.26) and Peter while on the roof of Simon the tanner "fell into a trance" (Acts 10:10). Likewise, both Paul and John fell into trances. In 2 Corinthians 12.1-4, Paul describes an experience where he didn't know if he was in his body or not. He was caught up where he heard inexpressible things that he was not permitted to tell. The experience is described as a vision/trance and not a dream. The implication is that Paul was immobile during the experience (2 Corinthians 12:1). This implies that he was awake when the revelation came and that for whatever time the experience lasted he was in some sort of trance-like state, most likely in a prone position. When John received the revelation of Jesus Christ in a visionary experience, he wrote, "When I saw Him I <u>fell at his feet as though dead</u>" (Revelation 1:17). This indicates that John was immobile.

This kind of experience is not solely contained in the first century, but has occurred numerous times throughout the history of the church. Jonathan Edwards, a theologian of the Great Awakening in America (1725-1760),says in his Account of the Revival of Religion in Northhampton 1740-1742 that "Many have had their religious affections raised far beyond what they had ever been before; and there were some instances of persons *lying in a sort of trance, remaining perhaps for a whole twenty-four hours motionless, and with their muscles locked up*

138

[my emphasis]." He goes on to say "there were some [were] so affected, and their *bodies so overcome* [my emphasis], that they could not go home, but were *obligated to stay all night where they were* [my emphasis]"(renewaljournal.wordpress.com).   The revivalist Charles Finney (1792-1875) gave an address in which he described the condition of Sodom, before God destroyed it. He states:

> I had not spoken in this strain more than a quarter of an hour, ' says he, 'when an awful solemnity seemed to settle upon them, the <u>congregation began to fall from their seats in every direction</u>, and cried for mercy. If I had a sword in each hand I could not have cut them down as fast as they fell. Nearly the whole congregation were either on their knees or prostrate, I should think, in less than two minutes from the shock that fell upon them. Every one prayed who was able to speak at all. ' Similar scenes were witnessed in many other places. (renewaljournal.wordpress. com)

In Summary, a pattern emerges from both the scriptures and church history that portrays "falling down" as a normal response to encountering the presence of God or his messengers. Sometimes

139

the Holy Spirit caused people to drop to the ground in holy fear (fear of the Lord) instead of working on them for some spiritual reason.

Interestingly, the majority of biblical men fell face down. The kinds of falling we are seeing now seem to parallel more the action of God to immobilize for the purpose of divine intervention, or rest and healing, rather than contrition. While some fall face down, the most people fall backwards.

I have seen this phenomenon hundreds of times. When I first saw it happen, even after my "filling" with the Holy Spirit, I thought it was kind of hokey. I asked myself: Why do people have to do that? I did not understand that they were not falling on purpose (although sometimes I think in some Charismatic churches it is customary to fall-what jokingly is referred to as a "courtesy fall", so the minister won't feel bad about nothing happening). As this revival was occurring in my Baptist congregation, I had no frame of reference for what was going on. At the end of the revival, Rick Godwin prayed for me at the front (the sermon had been odd in the sense it seemed to be a pastoral charge to me). I began to feel this sinking sensation inside of me, as if all my strength was leaking out my toes. When this feeling descended past my waist, I knew that I was going to be unable to stand, so I backed up and sat down on the front pew. I fell over prone on the pew, and I could not move. I could not get up, and the services ended and the guest left. I was disturbed that I could not do my pastoral duties. While I lay there, the Lord told me that He didn't need me to be the "pastor" of the church; He was THE pastor of the church, and my own strength was not what was needed. Later, a man offered me his hand and pulled me up. I never again questioned the "purpose" of falling down; since that time, I have experienced scores of this kind of experience.[56]

---

56 I was serving as a catcher when Charles Hunter mistakenly thought I was in line for ministry. He touched my forehead and an explosion of white light went off in my sight; I dropped immediately like a rock. Someone pulled me up and I felt like I was drunk in the Spirit. Another time, I fell out of my front row seat and was so immobilized (barely breathing and a sense of sinking through the floor) that began to enter into some kind of vision/trance as if I were going into heaven. During that same revival, I was immobilized on the floor around 11:30 pm. As associate pastor, I told them I would lock up after the experience was over. After what I thought was 30-40 minutes, I got up at 2:20 in the morning. I had completely lost track of time during the experience. More recently (June 2014), two Aussies prayed for me and I was immobilized for an hour and a half. During that time, I was receiving revelation about my life (my spiritual status with the Lord which had become a little "dry" and other reminders and

Shaking

Shaking or Quaking (associated with the Shakers and the Quakers in the western expansion period of the United States) is sometimes called trembling in the scriptures. There are many verses that relate to this phenomenon. For example, in Dan.10:7 Daniel states, "I, Daniel, alone saw the vision. For the men who were with me did not see the vision. But a great quaking/*trembling fell* [my emphasis] on them so that they fled to hide themselves." In fact, this is the kind of response shows up repeatedly during an encounter with the Lord God. The following verses support this assertion: Ps. 99:1-- 1. The Lord reigns, let the nations tremble; he sits enthroned between the cherubim, let the earth shake; " 2. Ps. 114:7: "Tremble O earth at the presence of the Lord;" 3. Acts 4.31: "The place where they were meeting was shaken;" and 4. Jer.23.9: In speaking of his prophetic experience, Jeremiah says, "My heart is broken within me; all my bones tremble.

---

encouragement). More significantly, while I was on the floor I felt a prick/sting on the bend of my right arm. In my mind I had a vision of an angel hooking me up to an IV for hydration. I then felt pressure on my head as if he were taking my spiritual temperature. There is more. But that is enough to make this point.

I am like a drunk man overcome by wine because of the Lord and his holy words." The text implies that Jeremiah was shaking from the inside out.

Jeremiah 23:9 is a significant verse because Jeremiah is relating what happened to him on at least one occasion involved a trembling/shaking of his bones. His wording seems to imply that he shook from the inside out. It would take a powerful force to cause his bones to quiver inside his body. The analogy to being overcome could also be a reference to being seized by the coming of the prophetic word. This text is a response to God's plea in Jeremiah 5: 22 which states, "Should you not fear me?" declares the LORD. "Should you not tremble in my presence?"

George Fox, the founder of the Quakers, wrote: "The Lord's power began to shake them and great meetings we began to have, and a mighty power and work of God there was amongst people, to the astonishment of both people and priests . . . After this I went to Mansfield, where there was a great meeting of professors and people; here I was moved to pray, and the Lord's power was so great, that the house seemed to be shaken." On another occasion, Fox states, "The priest scoffed at us and called us 'Quakers.' But the Lord's power was so over them and the word of life was declared in such authority and dread to them, that <u>the priest began trembling himself</u>; and one of the people said, 'Look how the priest trembles and shakes, he is turned Quaker also" (renewaljournal.wordpress.com).

To summarize, there is a biblical precedent for shaking in God's presence. In some of the previous verses where the cause of shaking is mentioned the subjects experience a holy fear. Some shaking, however, relates simply to the nature of the power of God visiting human flesh. Mountains shook when God touched down upon them, how much more so if he should touch human flesh. The times I have shook or supernaturally trembled in response to the power of the Holy Spirit has mostly occurred during worship. As I sensed the presence of the Holy Spirit growing on/in me I would stop singing and begin to speak lowly in tongues. As His power increased, I would extend my hands outward as if I were on a cross. Suddenly the power of God would hit me, and I would start shaking or trembling.

Drunkenness

In Ephesians 5:8, Paul exhorts the Ephesians to put off their old lifestyle, "Do not get drunk on wine which leads to debauchery, Instead, be filled (Greek present tense: Keep on being filled) with the Holy Spirit." Paul is contrasting the effects of two

144

kinds of drunkenness-one natural and one spiritual. The sense of the passage suggests a kind of Hebrew parallelism, yet with a contrastive purpose. Being filled with God's Spirit is similar to being drunk on wine. The primary difference is that the former is holy while the other is sinful.

An incident exemplifying this passage is found in Acts 2:13 where Peter and the upper room disciples poured out onto the street under the power of the Holy Spirit. Those that saw them believed that the disciples however were drunk, saying". . .They have had too much wine." Peter goes on to say, "These men are not drunk as you suppose. It is only nine in the morning! No, this is what was spoken by the prophet Joel: 'In the last days I will pour out my Spirit.'" Apparently the 120 upper room believers were acting in a drunken manner after being baptized in the Holy Spirit or with fire. This is what is known as an argument from silence. The text never says that they were drunk, but it is inferred. They would not be accused of being drunk because they were speaking in different languages. They would have been accused of such behavior because they were acting like drunks, i.e., laughing, falling, affected speech by some, boldness through lack of restraint, etc. The analogy of the gift of the Spirit being "new wine" would lend itself to the connection (See Jer. 23:9- I am like a drunken man, like a strong man overcome by wine, because of the LORD and his holy words.

In summary, while there are a limited number of passages on being drunk in the Spirit, the phenomenon is addressed in the scripture and experiences in revival meetings seem to support such manifestations.

Crying

Crying is an evangelically approved manifestation of the Holy Spirit, often connected with repentance from sin. I do not include it here because I think evangelicals need scriptural proof that crying can indicate the touch or ministry of the Holy Spirit. I include this phenomenon to suggest that Evangelicals are familiar with some manifestations of the Holy Spirit that are more acceptable in their culture. Verses that support crying as a result of conviction include: Nehemiah 8.9, " All the people had been weeping as they listened to the words of the law;" Chronicles 34:27, "Because your heart was responsive and you humbled yourself... and you tore your robes and wept in my presence I have heard you;" and Acts 2.37: "When the people heard this, they were cut to the heart..." *While this passage doesn't say they wept, "being cut to the heart" suggests that there may have been the emotional response.*

146

Additionally, John Wesley, founder of the Methodists, records how the Holy Spirit convicted the people in Bristol on *April 17, 1739 when he preached on the power of the Holy Spirit in Acts 4.* He states,

> We then called upon God to confirm His Word, immediately one that stood by (to our no small surprise) cried out aloud, with the utmost,' vehemence, even as the agonies of death. But we continued in prayer, till 'a new song was put in her mouth, a thanksgiving unto our God. ' Soon after, two other persons (well known in this place, as laboring to live in all good conscience towards all men were seized with strong pain, and constrained **to roar** for the disquietness of their heart. These also found peace. Many other wonderful cases of conviction of sin attended Wesley's preaching. It was a frequent occurrence for people **to cry aloud or fall down [my emphasis]** as if dead in the meetings, so great was their anguish of heart, caused, no doubt, by the Holy Spirit convicting them of sin. (Lawson, *Deeper Experiences of Famous Christians*)

The Role of Manifestations

In Short, crying is a natural and normal response to the conviction or ministry of the Holy Spirit (to release grief, bring repentance or as a sign of joy.)

Laughter

While there are not a lot of texts that describe laughter as a manifestation, this reaction is mostly associated with joy (or in some cases spiritual drunkenness). Some of these verses seem to apply: Ps.126:2,5 " Our mouths were filled with laughter, our tongues with songs of joy.... those who sow in tears will reap in joy;" Ps. 2:4 states, "The One enthroned in heaven laughs; the Lord scoffs at them" (If God laughs in heaven, he surely can laugh in us, particularly at the schemes of the enemy or when we are filled with joy).[57] When the 72 disciples return

---

57 Our ministry team was performing inner healing and deliverance for a woman who had been sexually abused for a number of years by relatives and then later raped. When she tried to offer forgiveness to them, she went back into the memory and started wailing and curling up into a fetal position. I brought her out of the cycling by asking her to look at me and leading her to forgive them. At the end of the profession of forgiveness, something remarkable happened. All of a sudden, she started to laugh uncontrollably; she was free. Her countenance was lighter. To this day, this is the most remarkable, "turn on a

declaring that even the demons were subject to them, Jesus was filled with joy (in the Greek akin to danced (twirled) with joy (Luke 10:21 -- At that time Jesus, full of joy through the Holy Spirit, said, "I praise you, Father, Lord of heaven and earth, because you have hidden these things from the wise and learned, and revealed them to little children. Yes, Father, for this is what you were pleased to do). It is logically, and by nature, hard to believe that being "filled with joy" does not include, at least the possibility, of laughter (John 17:13, "I am coming to you now but I say these things while I am still in the world so that they may have *the full measure of my joy within them* [my emphasis].") Additional evidence is found in the First Great Awakening and some subsequent revivals. Jonathan Edwards referring to this time states:

> It was very wonderful to see how person's affection were sometimes moved....Their joyful surprise has caused their hearts as it were to leap, so that they have been made *ready to break forth into laughter,* [my emphasis] tears often at the same time

---

dime" transformation that I have ever witnessed. She went from a wailing, terrified despair to ecstatic joy expressed through laughter. This memory has sustained me in this ministry of the Holy Spirit.

> issuing like a flood, and intermingling a loud
> weeping. Sometimes they have not been
> able to forebear crying out with a loud voice,
> expressing their great admiration.

In more recent times, laughter has characterized particularly the ministry of Evangelist Rodney Howard Browne and the "Toronto Blessing" revival at John Arnott's church (formerly called the Toronto Airport Vineyard) in the early to mid-nineties. Conclusion: Again, laughter fits within the general flow of Scripture. Christians can be so filled with the joy of the Lord that they are given over to fits of laughter.

Less Noticeable and Extra-Biblical Manifestations

There are some manifestations in the operation of the ministry of the Holy Spirit that are implied or at least logical in regard to other manifestations of the Holy Spirit mentioned in the Bible. One common manifestation is heat or a feeling of burning. This manifestation is not as noticeable because it is less visible to others. The only visibility might be that the person is turning red in the face or hands, or he or she begins to fan himself or herself as if he or she is having a "hot flash" (you need to be sure you don't jump to any spiritual conclusion when this phenomenon is attributed to women who might be experiencing menopause). The Holy Spirit and God are described as fire, so it is logical to assume that there is certain manifestations associated with heat/burning. Jeremiah stated in Jer. 20:9, "But if I say, "I will not mention his word or speak anymore in his name," his word is in my heart like a fire, a *fire shut up in my bones* [my emphasis].[58] I am weary of holding it in; indeed, I cannot." He states in Lamentations 1:13a "*From on high he sent fire* [my emphasis], sent it down into my bones."

On numerous occasions our church (Wind and Fire Church) has experienced the phenomenon of heat (even a wind blew into our fellowship coming from three different directions in three square feet of where three of us were standing, but that is a story for another time). Sometimes numerous people feel hot as the Holy Spirit moves in a fellowship, or the heat may be localized in someone's hands. This manifestation is indicative of the power of the Holy Spirit becoming available for the ministry of the laying on of hands. Heat is usually associated with physical healing, and people who are being healed will sometimes feel hot all over or hot in the area

---

58 Jeremiah 23:29 states, "'Is not my word like fire [my emphasis],' declares the Lord, 'and like a hammer that breaks a rock in pieces?'"

where someone is placing his or her hand or the healing is manifesting.

A tingling sensation is logically supported based on other phenomena, even though it is less supported in scripture (Jer. 19:3–"His ears shall tingle"). This sensation, which I usually experience on my hands, appears to be a neurological phenomenon. This is consistent with "immobilization," when people cannot get up off the floor, sometimes for hours. Simply, the brain cannot will the body to do anything. It is also possible that tingling is associated with heat because the nerves convey this particular sensation to the brain and it is identified as heat. For me, the tingling sensation is connected to God's power and is an indication that the Holy Spirit is present, or He is interested in healing someone. Sometimes people who are being prompted by the gift of tongues or prophecy will notice that their lips will tingle.

Environmental Manifestations

While I have not experienced these phenomena, they are said to have occurred in some churches: a mist or a light that highlights someone. When Solomon's temple was dedicated it is recorded that a cloud filled the temple. 2 Chronicles 5: 13-14 reads:

"[13] The trumpeters and musicians joined
in unison to give praise and thanks to
the LORD. Accompanied by trumpets,
cymbals and other instruments, the singers
raised their voices in praise to the LORD and
sang:

"He is good;
his love endures forever."

Then the temple of the LORD was filled with
the cloud, [14] and the priests could
not perform their service because of the
cloud, for the glory of the LORD filled the
temple of God.

Here we see that God's glory is associated
with a cloud (water vapor) or a mist. In this case
it is so dense that the priests could not minister or
they had fallen and were immobilized. In addition
to a mist there is also light. The appearance of a
light at the moment of Saul's conversion is found in
Acts 9:3 ([3] As he neared Damascus on his journey,
suddenly a light from heaven flashed around him).
These manifestations are rare, as well as other more
miraculous and substantive manifestations.[59] The

---

59 I have been in meetings where people received gold
teeth, i.e., one or more of their teeth have turned to

latter group of manifestations such as gold teeth and gold dust etc are, for the most part, miracles that are possible but are not recorded in the scripture.

---

gold. Additionally, I have seen gold dust and have heard about other phenomena occurring as "signs" of God's presence.

Chapter Nine: Experiential Religion: The Heritage of Evangelicalism

Many denominations began as movements that challenged the paradigm of previously existing denominations but are now finding themselves either in decline or in a struggle to remain relevant to the deeper needs of people. Movements grow rapidly and bring spiritual fervor to their new coverts; unfortunately, as the movement gets larger there is an attempt to conserve its gains by putting into place traditions that are based on the common spiritual narrative of the group, but lacks the prior fervor and pursuit of God. Since the establishing of new orthodox spiritual movements are through the impetus of the Holy Spirit, the lack of fervor is attributed to the reduced influence of the Holy Spirit in the group. As His influence lessens, faith begins to falter and the Holy Spirit's activity is replaced by doctrines and practices that are managed by the human intellect and are based on natural talents.

An example of this is found in the life of

Experiential Religion: The Heritage of Evangelicalism

Gideon. Gideon was called to be a judge (deliverer) in Israel in order to rescue them from the oppression of the Midianites. As the story goes, Gideon succeeded because "the Lord was with him." The judges were "charismatic" or especially chosen leaders who were raised up for a certain time of crisis, and then they were supposed to return to their normal occupation, because Israel did not have a king. Their king was God, himself. Unfortunately, Gideon's ephod was placed on a pole and was considered a sacred object for the people, who came and worshiped it. Gideon not only started this idolatry, but also permitted people to engage in this forbidden practice. The ephod represented what God had done through a man (human agency), and instead of depending on God for whatever new direction he would provide they celebrated the spent glory of their past. Many denominations of today began as a movement lead by the Holy Spirit, yet those same denominations have lost the vigor of the Holy Spirit's activity and are now trusting in methods and doctrines, while they do the work of the ministry under their own power.

Additionally, these denominations (movements) began usually among the poor of society, which means they were less educated and without the resources of those in a higher economic strata. Both of these factors reflect two particular

qualities that sociologically inform the emergence
of religious movements and also cause those same
movements to loss their vitality. First, simplicity in
thought, in regard to a lack of intellectual processes
that contribute to an increase in doubt, is a
characteristic more in keeping with those that are
less educated. This tends to be the critical mantra
used against the less educated by "liberal" educated
people to suggest that the Christian faith is akin to
superstition or ignorance. In fact, a study conducted
a few decades ago[60] of those who are seminary
educated or who have attended institutions of higher
learning and have done work in the field of religious
studies show that these individuals suffer a loss of
confidence in the scriptures and the more orthodox
views of their denominations. It seems that the role of
graduate work in the field of Christianity and religious
studies involves a certain amount of skepticism and
modernism reflected in "Higher" Criticism of the
biblical text. That is why Jesus commends the faith of
little children and suggests entrance into the kingdom
is based on that faith. Certainly little children are not
noted for their intellectual prowess. That is not to

---

60 There has been a shift in certain evangelical seminaries
to a more conservative posture regarding the scriptures in
the last two decades.

say, we should become anti-intellectual.

Second, those who are poor tend to trust in God more than in their bank account for resources. Early Christianity was criticized by one Roman writer who described its patrons as the riff-raff of Rome. This is in keeping with the sociological idea that "new" religions begin with the less educated (who are often the poorest in a society). Because the poor in most nations greatly outnumber the rich or upper middle-class, they form a ready base for the quick expansion of any new religion, cult or sect of Christianity. Sociologists and church growth specialists note that there is an upward mobility of the poor when they become converted to Christ. Christianity provides the necessary motivations for a new convert to begin a socio-economic rise in status. While this may be seen in other religions that have a strong moral code, my focus is on Christianity. This rise in socio-economic status is a benefit to the convert, but also carries some unintended consequences. The benefits are obvious: conversion to Christ means a rejection of all the vices that drain economic resources; marital and family relationships are repaired, which results in domestic stability; Christianity instills a sense of purpose/destiny and enhances the sense of work ethic and moral responsibility to provide for the family; and inclusion in a supportive community

158

results in encouragement to succeed, financial assistance when necessary, and opens the door to new networking possibilities. However, there are negative unintended consequences regarding the upward mobility of the members of a particular denomination. Such consequences are as follows: 1. A church that is pulled into a more materialistic pursuit of the "American Dream;" 2. The reduction in the association with the poor, who are the most open to the gospel of Jesus Christ; 3. A greater sense of homogeneity (only associating with people who are just like us); 4. The conforming to a consensus idea of what a dignified appropriate decorum should be for someone who is a professional, upwardly mobile, member of a social class that considers outward appearance, in keeping with one's status, important. It is this last point that is most detrimental to allowing the Holy Spirit to do whatever he desires to do within the context of any church service. The lack of dignity regarding some manifestations of the Holy Spirit is an affront to those who have achieved the status of respect because of their economic position in the community. Furthermore, even if a person did value the actions of the Holy Spirit, there is a reluctance to invite one's friends to attend or be a part of a service that is contrary to the respectability engendered by their economic status. Likewise, there's a tendency not to involve highly educated people in a church where they have to associate with people less educated. When they say "birds of feather flock together" that is just a popular way of affirming the principle of hegemony/homogeneous association. The appeal to welcoming the professional class as part of one's congregation is obvious—greater financial resources. That is not to say that this socio-economic group is "*ipso facto*" opposed to the Holy Spirit and his ministry. There are plenty of exceptions to this observation. However, by now, you might want to know: What is your point? My point is simple: Denominations that began among the poor with a passion for Jesus, openness to the Holy Spirit, and a commitment to reaching the lost, begin to move away from the spiritual fervor that marked their denomination as they began to grow in their socio-economic status as a denomination. They lost the very dynamic that caused them to be a vibrant fast-growing denomination. Once again, there are exceptions to this general assertion. At this point, it is helpful to remind evangelical denominations of their heritage. To this end, I will concentrate on the revival history of evangelicals.

A good resource regarding the formation of the Evangelical character is Nancey Pearcey's *Total Truth: Liberating Christianity from Its Cultural*

Captivity (Wheaton, IL:Crossway Books/Good News P, 2004). Pearcey laments the anti-intellectual tradition that influenced/birthed evangelicalism, but behind this concern there is an important sub-text of which evangelicals need to be reminded. Pearcey maintains, "Historically, evangelicalism began as a renewal movement within the churches, not as a separate denomination – and that explains why at first it did not develop an independent intellectual tradition. . . Their goal was to cultivate a *subjective* experience of *objective* biblical truths"(253). This is exactly the goal of the Charismatics regarding experience and the scripture. Furthermore, like evangelicalism, the Charismatic movement began as a movement within churches. According to Pearcey, "evangelicalism grew the First and Second Great Awakenings, embracing a revivalist style of preaching and an emphasis on personal conversion ("the New Birth")" (256). While the result of the two Great Awakenings was conversions, she does not mention the attendant activities of the Holy Spirit, which were a variety of manifestations of the Holy Spirit. Pearcey goes on to state, "Thus the rhetoric of revival tended to have an anti-authoritarian and anti-traditionalist flavor, denouncing liturgy and ceremonies as empty, external ritualism" (257). Interestingly enough, the same charges were sometimes leveled at the charismatic movement during the 60s and 70s by those who did not welcome the Holy Spirit and his activities as expressed by the anti-authoritarian and anti-traditionalist flavor of its adherents. It seems that any new movement is always opposed by the established order. The mainline churches of the 1700s in America (Old Lights-a term given to them by the emerging evangelicals) opposed the revival that was taking place under the ministry of Jonathan Edwards and George Whitefield. "When the First and Second Great Awakenings broke out, the liberal clergy firmly opposed them, declaring themselves on the side of 'Reason' against the revivalist 'religion of a heart'"(261). Pearcey notes,

> Religious organizations are stronger to the degree that they impose significant costs in terms of sacrifice and even stigma upon their members,' write Finke and Stark. Why? Because religions that demand a lot also give a lot. A, frankly, supernatural religion may demand more from adherents than a watered-down gospel of 'reasonable religion' or social activism. But in turm gives much greater rewards in terms of doctrinal substance, intense spiritual experience, and a sense of direct access to God. (261-62)

Pearcey laments that "Evangelical preachers broke with the older pattern of using sermons to instruct, and began to use their service to press hearers to a point of crisis, in order to produce a conversion experience" (263). The entire point of Pearcey's book is to assert that Evangelicals became anti-intellectual to appeal to the emotions of the lost in order to win more souls to Jesus, ignoring the fact that those churches who were the most intellectual of their day opposed the personal appeal of the heart-felt religion (and its "invitation" to decision) in a favor of a slower intellectual process. They were interested in nurturing a person into faith as opposed to forcing a person into a crisis regarding the acceptance of Jesus as savior. "Supporters of the Awakening [Evangelicals] insisted that a merely intellectual assent to theological propositions was not enough. What was needed was a 'Change of Heart' or a 'New Birth' (Pearcey 269). Ironically, Evangelicals were promoting experiences over the intellectual acceptance of good doctrine. Apparently, it was okay for Evangelicals to promote a salvation experience, whatever that looked like (even today, no one knows for sure whether or not a person is saved just by looking at him), but it is risky to permit Charismatics/ Pentecostals to indulge in promoting a spiritual experience that is also represented in the

Bible. "'Our people do not need so much as to have
their heads stored, as to have their hearts touched'
wrote Jonathan Edwards [considered an American
Calvinist <u>genius</u> by historians] the preeminent
theorist of the First Great Awakening, in 1743. One
of his protégés described the best preacher as one
'whose heart is ravished with the glory of divine
things'" (Pearcey 269).

The history of revival in America has
always included those who stood in opposition to
these seasons of renewal. In some cases, a specific
individual can be identified as having almost single-
handedly shut down moves of God for the sake of
"saving" the church from error. The First Great
Awakening is a case in point. During the time of
Jonathan Edwards, toward the end of 1734, the
revival broke out in Northhampton. At that time
worldliness and a lack of spiritual interest had
reached a high level in the colonies. Deism, imported
from Europe, was replacing the more orthodox view
represented by Calvinism.[61] Two years later some

---

61 Deism maintained that God created everything but he is
no longer involved in his creation. Hence, He no longer, if
ever, did miracles, communicated with people, or could be
counted on to intervene in human affairs. Sound familiar?
Deism is an early form of Cessationism, and it led to
worldliness and an ebbing of the Christian Faith.

300 persons had received Christ as Savior. Historians record the virtues of the revival, while admitting that there were emotional excesses that took place. Jonathan Edwards, in addressing these excesses, wrote a treatise/sermon entitled *The Distinguishing Marks of a Work of the Spirit of God*. In this sermon, Edwards provides a guide for determining whether or not a revival is a legitimate expression of the Spirit of God.[62] Despite his efforts to bring correction to the movement and steward the results of the revival, there were those who desired to shut the revival down. Foremost in attacking the revival--and its various leaders including George Whitfield, James Davenport (an extremist), and Gilbert Tennent (an extremist)-- was Charles Chauncy, associate pastor of First Church of Boston. Chauncy was methodical

---

62 Edwards was concerned with the results of the revival more so than its particular manifestations. So he lists the following attributes of what constitutes a revival by the Spirit of God. He suggests the following characteristics: "1. [It] raises the esteem of Jesus in the community, proclaiming him as Scripture depicts them, son of God and Savior; 2. [It] works against the kingdom of Satan, which encourages sin and worldly lusts; 3. [It] stimulates 'a greater regard for the Holy Scriptures, and establishes them more in their truth and divinity'; 4. [It] is marked by a spirit of truth; and] 5. [It] manifests a renewed love of God and man" (DeArteaga 43).

in his lifestyle to the point of being obsessive-compulsive and was uncomfortable with the expression of emotion (DeArteaga 45-46). This was one of the most troubling aspects of the revival in his estimation; he viewed the manifestations of the Holy Spirit as simply worked up emotions exhibited through people who were whipped into a frenzy by extemporaneous preachers, who challenged the norm of ministry and decorum. When extremist James Davenport, who somehow thought that God had appointed him to determine whether or not a person was actually saved (similar to those who feel appointed by God to determine who is in doctrinal error), challenged Chauncey, Chauncey was further resolved to oppose the revival. Chauncey went on to publish a point by point refutation of Edward's *Some Thoughts Concerning Revival* (DeArteaga 52). His work *Seasonable Thoughts on the State of Religion in New England* became a best seller and marked the end of the Awakening (DeArteaga 52). The benefits of the First Great Awakening are unquestionable. The First Great Awakening shaped the character of evangelical Christianity (as a born again heart-felt religion), prepared the colonists in their separation from England, contributed to the formation of most of the Ivy League universities, and resulted in a phenomenal increase of churches and new converts.

166

"From 1740 to 1742 the awakening has [*sic*] swept 25,000 to 50,000 members into the new England churches alone, between 1750 in 1760, 150 new Congregational bodies were formed, to say nothing of the steadily proliferating Baptists" (Shelley 349). It is more likely that people have heard of Jonathan Edwards, who is considered one of the early American geniuses, but few, if any, have heard of Charles Chauncy. Edwards went on to become president of Princeton in 1757, while Chauncy "became one of the founding theologians of Unitarianism, the American Deistic cult" (DeArteaga 53). Unitarianism denies the deity of Christ, the Trinity (hence a denial of the Holy Spirit) and, according to the apostle John in 1 John, is considered an expression of the spirit of anti-Christ. It seems there's not much difference between a staunch conservative denier of the work of the Holy Spirit and being a member of a Unitarian "church." [Hmmm, that may be a tad unfair if not a faulty analogy. However, it is something to think about.]. The First Great Awakening was followed by the Second Great Awakening.

Pearcey goes on to recount similar sentiments regarding the need for heart-felt religion found in the Second Great Awakening, the one that saw a marked increase in membership among Baptists and especially Methodists. She states:

167

Experiential Religion: The Heritage of Evangelicalism

> Consider a *typical* [my emphasis] conversion account from very early in the second Awakening. James McGready was studying for the Presbyterian ministry when it struck him that, even though his theological beliefs were orthodox and his moral behavior impeccable, these things were not enough. 'When he came to examine *his feelings* [Pearcey's emphasis], to try them by such passages as, being filled with the spirit; filled with joy; filled with the Holy Ghost; joy of the Holy Ghost. . .,' it seemed to him that he did not understand these things experimentally' wrote an early historian. (Pearcey 269-70)

Documents from Robert A. Baker's *A Baptist Source Book* (Nashville: Broadman P, 1996) provide primary source documents written in the time period of the Second Great Awakening. Many of the writers were first-hand witnesses of what occurred in the revivals. As a preface to these writings, it should be noted that the perspective is from Baptists who were not necessarily in favor of everything they witnessed. My point here is: manifestations of the Holy Spirit during a period of revival occurred before the formation of the Pentecostal denomination or the emergence of the Charismatic movement.

Neither groups unleashed what is considered excesses of "spiritual frenzy" on the Christian church at large. Such "phenomena" were a part of Baptist, Presbyterian, and Methodist experience, like it or not. With this caveat in place, we will proceed.

At least one prominent Baptist, Shubal Stearns, during the period of the First Great Awakening, benefited from the moving of the Holy Spirit in his preaching.[63] An attendee of one of Rev. Stearns meetings, a Mr. Tidence Lane, reports, "when he began to preach, my perturbations increased, so that nature could no longer support them, and I sunk to the ground" (qtd. by Baker 18).[64]

Baker includes a report on the "Revival in North Carolina (Sandy Creek Assoc.)" by the Rev. George Pope, the pastor of the church at Abbot's Creek, to Benedict.

In the progress of the revival among Baptists,

---

63 Another Baptist, Isaac Backus, a defender of religious freedom, was converted in 1741 during the Great Awakening. He became a Baptist in 1751. Founded a Baptist congregation at Middleboro, Mass., in 1756 and served as its pastor until his death (www.reformedreader.org/backus). The fruit of the rowdy Awakening benefited not just congregationalists.

64 From Morgan Edwards in Materials.

and, especially, at their camp meetings, there were exhibited scenes of the most solemn and affecting nature; and in many instances there was heard at the same time, throughout the congregation, a mingled sound of prayer, exhortation, groans, and praise. The fantastic exercise of jerking, dancing &c [*sic*] in a religious way, prevailed much with the united body of Methodists and Presbyterians, towards the close of the revival; but they were not introduced at all among the Baptists in these parts. But falling down under religious impressions was frequent among them. Many were taken with these religious epilepsies, if we may so call them, not only at the great meetings, where those scenes were exhibited, which were calculated to move the sympathetic affections, but also about their daily employments, some in the fields, some in their houses, and some hunting their cattle in the woods. And in some cases, people were thus strangely affected when alone; so that if some played the hypocrite, with others the exercise must have been voluntary and unaffected. And besides falling down, there were many other expressions of zeal, which in more moderate people would be considered enthusiastic and wild.

The above relation was given me by Rev. George Pope, the pastor of the church at Abbot's Creek, who is a man of sense and moderation, and who, with many of his brethren, was much tried in his mind, and stood aloof from the work at its commencement; but it spread so rapidly and powerfully, that they soon discovered such *evident marks of its being a genuine work of grace, notwithstanding its new and unusual appearances* [my emphasis] that their doubts subsided, and they cordially and zealously engaged in forwarding and promoting it. Mr. Pope, in the course of the revival baptized about 500 persons. (Benedict op cite 1813 II 251-252 qtd. by Baker 47)

Here we see a "man of sense and moderation" whose original approach to the revival with its unusual manifestations of the Spirit was one of skepticism until he saw the "fruit" or results of the revival, which was an increase in conversions and a devotion to Jesus Christ (the latter is implied).

David Lilly in a letter dated August 23, 1802 recounts the revival in South Carolina stating,

I take my pen in hand to transmit to you

> good tidings. A *great work of God is going on* [my emphasis] in the upper parts of this state. Multitudes are made to cry out, 'What shall we do to be saved' . . . Then the Lord was pleased to manifest his power to many hearts. Numbers were powerfully exercised through the whole night, and *some were thrown to the ground* [a typical biblical manifestation of the Holy Spirit—see chapter eight).
>
> On Monday the work increased. The hearts of many were made to melt; and several men, noted for their impiety, were stricken and *lay among the prostrate* [see previous note]. (From Georgia Analytical Repository Vol. I number 3 qtd. by Baker 49)

Lilly's report is interesting for at least two reasons: 1. He considers the results of the revival, i.e., the conversion of souls as particularly indicative of a work of God, and 2. The manifestations of the Holy Spirit, including the affect it had on lost people or the impious, are considered acceptable expressions of the work of the Holy Spirit. It should be noted that these manifestations occurred among denominations that are considered evangelical. While David Lilly might be unfamiliar among some Baptists, Richard Furman, who has a Baptist University named after him, also wrote about the Second Great Awakening.[65]

While Furman neither affirms or disaffirms the manifestations of the Holy Spirit during the revival, he does record the positive effects of the revival. Referring to a joint revival meeting with Baptists, Presbyterians and Methodists in attendance, he states,

> Some of them *fell instantly*, as though struck with lightning, and continued *insensible for a length of time* [my emphasis]; others were more mildly affected, and soon their bodily

---

65 "Unlike some of his Baptist brethren who viewed formal theological training as an impediment to true religion and the moving of the Holy Spirit, Furman was a keen advocate of an educated ministry. He founded Columbian College (modern-day George Washington University) in 1821 (fittingly, the South's first Baptist college, Furman University, was posthumously named in his honor). . . . Furman's activities in South Carolina led to the founding of the South Carolina Baptist Convention (he served as its first president from 1821 to 1825), the first state Baptist convention in the United States and a template for the formation and administration of the future Southern Baptist Convention (1845)." (taken from Wheaton College-Institute for the Study of American Evangelicals; http://www.wheaton.edu/isae/hall-of-biography/richard-furman).

> strength, with proper command of their mental powers. Deep conviction for sin, and apprehension of the wraith [*sic*] of God, was professed by the chief of them at first; and several of them afterwards appeared to have a joyful sense of pardoning mercy through a redeemer. (Letter from Richard Furman dated August 11, 1802—from Benedict [1813] II, 188 qtd. by Baker 51)

Lacy K. Ford in *Origins of Southern Radicalism: The South Carolina Upcountry, 1800-1860* notes the following:

> The Holy Spirit, one Bethesda member recalled, 'passed through that vast assembly like some mighty whirlwind. The people were moved as the trees of wood [*sic*] are moved by the wind.' Converts were won 'from almost every age, character, class, and condition.' Largely as a result of this camp meeting, the Betheseda congregation grew from about 60 persons in 1802 to over 300 by 1805, as 'religion required [*sic*-acquired] an ascendency which it had not previously held' in the Bethesda area . . . The penetrating sighs and excruciating struggles of those under exercise, the grateful exhultations

[*sic*] of those brought to a sense of their guilty condition . . . were sufficient to bow the stubborn neck of infidelity . . . . Some are more easily and gently wrought and others . . . different stages from mild swoon to convulsive spasms may be seen"[66] (qtd. by Ford 26)

Ford records the tent meeting phenomena with its evangelism and church growth success; however, he notes that the character of the revival meetings was moderated by Presbyterians and Baptists because of the lack of doctrinal instruction that was taking place. The feeling was that either the "new" believers did not have the correct idea about "the nature of the gospel church" [possible code for not desiring to be a part of a particular minister's congregation] and sometimes they were given contradictory information at the camp meetings [e.g., Methodists were free-will and Presbyterians and Baptists tended to be Calvinistic] Additionally, Richard Furman was concerned that the free intercourse between the sexes [a reference

66 From A History of the Bethesda Presbyterian Church, pp. 79-87 in Bethesda Presbyterian Church records, SCL.

to conversation and "intermixing", not the more modern sexual understanding of the word] and the enthusiastic disposition was a matter to be criticized (Ford 27). Furthermore, the Baptists were concerned about preserving the integrity of the practice of closed communion—a practice which limits the taking of communion only with members of your own denomination, and sometimes, only with individuals of a particular Baptist church (Ford 27). Closed communion typified the rigid doctrine and practices of the Baptist church, which limited their cooperation and participation with other denominations in the revival movement. Having seen, however, the value of souls being won to Jesus both Baptists and Presbyterians modified (tamed?) the less palatable aspects of the revival they had witnessed. They wanted to "maintain a semblance of propriety and doctrinal orthodoxy" [orthodoxy according to their interpretations] so "Baptists and Presbyterians instituted a different revival form, the protracted meeting" (Ford 27).

> Protracted meetings were usually sponsored by an individual church and often held indoors . . . . protracted meetings normally attracted smaller crowds and were **easier to control** [my emphasis] than camp meetings, thus allowing the host church to monitor

revival teachings and congregational behavior more closely. Though open to all, protracted meetings were certainly more denominationally oriented than camp meetings, and , . . . marked a renewed emphasis on the winning of new members for specific churches . . . . Evangelism in the broadest sense was sacrificed, to some extent, to the more narrow aim of strengthening evangelical churches. (Ford 28)

These denominational protracted meetings [similar to the current tradition of having a week long or two week long revival] were effective in winning souls to Jesus, resulting in scores of salvations. However, it was noted by Elizabeth Cunningham's account of the Laurens revival of 1838 that there was a shift in producing a revival "in our Church" (qtd. by Ford 28). "Church building [building one's own congregation] now enjoyed nearly as much emphasis as soul saving in evangelical crusades" (Ford 28).
Ford notes:

As Donald G. Miller has pointed out, by the 1820s evangelical Christianity no longer concentrated solely on the salvation of lost souls, but instead devoted a healthy portion of its resources and **refinement of church institutions** [my emphasis], which more often than not were designed to nurture souls already saved [my question: Were they made into disciples or denominationalists?]. The regularization [making regular-an interesting choice of words] of the revival process [having revival meetings whether or not actual revival takes place] and **the increasing denominational control over all forms of revival** [my emphasis] were simply part of the process of institutional maturation and the concomitant emphasis on denominational distinctions within the evangelical movement. (29-30)

While Ford sees this change as a matter of maturation, I see it as a matter of domestication or routinization. Ford speaks as a historian, not as a professor of spiritual formation or church growth.

In summation, evangelical churches have their own history with the Holy Spirit that includes spiritual manifestations of the Holy Spirit prior to the formation of Pentecostal churches and the charismatic movement. While this history may be ignored or even suppressed, it nevertheless, was a part of the westward expansion and tremendous growth of evangelicals in the 1800s. To embrace the activity the Holy Spirit is not to become Pentecostal or even charismatic but instead is a return to the revivalistic practices of the camp meeting. Church history records that evangelicals were willing to put up with some oddities regarding the behavior of people under the influence of the Holy Spirit as long as people were being converted to Jesus and the end result was greater devotion to Jesus Christ. Why is there, then, a seemingly ingrained resistance among some evangelicals regarding the influence of the Holy Spirit?

Chapter 10: A Most Delicate and Disturbing Matter

Despite having a common interest in seeing the gospel of Jesus Christ and the Kingdom of God advance through the activity of the Holy Spirit, there has been a history of animosity, criticism, division, and accusation between those who wholeheartedly embrace a manifold expression of the Life of the Holy Spirit and those who desire to keep Jesus as central to the expression of their faith. The simple solution, in theory, is to embrace both within the discernment and leadership of the Holy Spirit. After all, one of the fruit of the Holy Spirit is self-control, i.e., the Holy Spirit keeps believers from acting out according to their fleshly desires and thinking patterns. Everyone can agree that violating Christ-like attitudes and a deficiency of the fruit of the Holy Spirit is a bad thing; it seems simple enough that with that agreement everyone should commit themselves to cultivating the virtues of Jesus and the fruit of the Spirit.

Additionally, it only seems reasonable that a passionate and strong desire to know Jesus more intimately would be supported by all Christians. If the methods used are biblical, have Christ-like results, and strengthens the church, why the intense opposition?

Now comes the delicate and disturbing matter, let's begin with an analogy. Where in the New Testament does the manifest coming of God's presence offend biblical traditionalists? The answer to that question is simple. The Pharisees opposed Jesus who is the revelation and manifest presence of God. In order to avoid a false analogy, it is very important to identify the characteristics that you are comparing. The Pharisees were the established religious order of their day. Evangelicalism is the established religious order of our day here in America. The Pharisees were strong Biblicists, i.e., they placed their trust in the authority of the Old Testament Scriptures just like most evangelicals place their trust in the Scriptures. In fairness, the Pharisees added additional laws and customs that were derived from the Scriptures and treated as just as authoritative. At this point, an evangelical might see the analogy breaking down. However, evangelicals have also added certain traditions as an application of the Scriptures. One particular denomination has something called a church covenant which states that its members shall not "engage in the use of or sale of alcohol." Other churches forbid dancing. Some churches are ruled by their congregations through a voting process. Clearly, there are certain practices and customs of evangelical churches that are seen as being based on Scripture but are simply an application of those Scriptures. This is what the Pharisees did. Jesus called their hand on their criticism of him and his disciples. Matthew records the encounter:

> Then some Pharisees and teachers of the law came to Jesus from Jerusalem and asked, ² "Why do your disciples break the tradition of the elders? They don't wash their hands before they eat!" ³ Jesus replied, "And why do you break the command of God for the sake of your tradition? ⁴ For God said, 'Honor your father and mother' and 'Anyone who curses their father or mother is to be put to death.' ⁵ But you say that if anyone declares that what might have been used to help their father or mother is 'devoted to God,' ⁶ they are not to 'honor their father or mother' with it. *Thus you nullify the word of God for the sake of your tradition* [my emphasis]. ⁷ You hypocrites! Isaiah was right when he prophesied about you:

[8] "'These people honor me with their lips,
but their hearts are far from me.
[9] They worship me in vain;
 their teachings are merely human rules [my emphasis].

How about, their teachings are merely humanly derived interpretations which nullify the intent and meaning of the word of God.

The Pharisees were a class of leaders that were set apart from the rest of the people, similar to the pastoral system that evangelicals have employed. Apparently, these religious leaders were highly trained in the Scriptures and their customs (seminary), were connected to the temple (church building), were considered by the people as their religious leaders, were considered as the best examples of righteousness, and they were looked to as the arbiters of religious truth in regard to what was considered Orthodox or heretical. Keep in mind there had not been a prophet in Israel for 400 years. The voice of God had remained silent. If you cannot hear God speaking, you will rely on what he has said rather than what he is saying. It is interesting to note that the last prophetic book listed in the Old Testament is Malachi, which speaks of the Elijah that is to come. Jesus refers to this Elijah as being John the Baptist who ministered in the spirit of Elijah. Consequently, the Pharisees had not seen any recognized/affirmed miraculous activity during their life-time, until Jesus came on the scene (John the Baptist performed no recorded miracles in the New Testament). There was nothing about their personal experience that validated miracles in their own ministry of teaching or "pastoral" care. Now, this assessment could be compared to any kind of religious leader of any denomination whether evangelical or not. The significance lies in the comparison between these religious leaders and their system of belief when they come into contact with Jesus. For the analogy to remain true and consistent, it is necessary to look at Jesus and what he meant to this religious system. First of all, Jesus was not trained in their "seminary" (rabbinical school) system, nor was he a member of the professional clergy (receiving money from the people who were faithful to the temple system) or located within the context of the temple (church building) although he attended the temple. So here's this carpenter's son, who is unendorsed by the religious system, has attracted a huge following, claims to hear and speak the voice of God, does miracles they have never seen before, which challenges their interpretation of the Scriptures, their desire to be honored and well-paid for their professional ministry, and their lack of humility. It is no wonder that they were angry with Jesus and decided to kill him. He upset their religious status quo. He spoke with authority because his words came from the Father, as opposed to simply repeating the interpretations of the Scripture (commentaries) handed down by previous rabbis. Instead of people listening to them and attending the temple where they ministered, they were following Jesus and supporting his ministry. They claimed he was divisive, but they were constantly arguing with him and challenging him in regard to his authority. The Pharisees discounted the truth that Jesus was saying, ignoring the miracles that he performed by suggesting that he performed those miracles through the activity if the devil. It was simple for them. If the doctrine wasn't right, then the miracles could not be from God. Basically, everything had to agree with them and their doctrine or it wasn't from God.

In John chapter 7, Jesus attends the Feast of Tabernacles. When he arrives there is mass confusion and division among the people. John 7:37-43 states:

> On the last day of the feast, the great day, Jesus stood up and cried out, 'if anyone thirsts, let him come to me and drink. Whoever believes in me, as the Scriptures has said, out of his heart will flow rivers of living water.' Now this he said about the

Spirit, whom those who believed in him were to receive, for as yet the Spirit had not been given, because Jesus was not yet glorified. When the people heard these words, some of the people said, 'This really is the prophet [Moses].' Others said, 'This is the Christ.' But some said, 'Is the Christ to come from Galilee?' *'Has not the Scriptures said* [my emphasis] that the Christ comes from the offspring of David, and comes from Bethlehem, the village where David was?' So there was division among the people over him.

First, I want you to notice that the people who did not believe in Christ used the scripture, but they did not know the truth regarding Jesus' origin, so they used the Scripture wrongly, which kept them from accepting Jesus. Second, Jesus causes the division among the people. Maybe, we should say Jesus presented the truth and it divided the people into two camps-those who believed in him and those who did not. It is not that Jesus was trying to be divisive, but the revelation he brought divided people. He is the Prince of Peace who was warred against, so there was no peace. This is exactly what he said would happen, when he stated:

Do not think that I have come to bring
peace   to the earth. I'm not come to
bring peace, but sword. I come to
set a man against his father, and a daughter
against her mother, and a daughter-in-law
against her mother-in-law. And a
person's enemies will be those of his own
household . . . . Whoever receive you
receives me, and whoever receives me
receives him who sent me.

Third, the context of Jesus speaking the words: "if anyone thirsts, let him come to me and drink. Whoever believes in me, as the Scriptures has said, out of his heart will flow rivers of living water" --which is the division and the confusion of the people regarding Jesus-- is the Feast of Tabernacles. In the Hebrew Scriptures, the Feast of Tabernacles is associated with the pouring of water on the altar and a great ingathering harvest. Typologically, this feast symbolizes a great end-time awakening that results in a tremendous number of souls being saved. When John says "now this he [Jesus] said about the Spirit," Pentecostals and some Charismatics believe Jesus was predicting the future coming of the Holy Spirit at Pentecost. Matthew 3:11-12 states, [11] "I baptize you with water for repentance. But after me comes one who is more powerful than I, whose sandals I am not worthy to carry. He will baptize you with the Holy Spirit and fire. [12] His winnowing fork is in his hand, and he will clear his threshing floor, gathering his wheat into the barn and burning up the chaff with unquenchable fire." Notice this is a reference to the coming of the Holy Spirit which is described as a baptism (we will discuss that later). There are two actions performed here by Jesus: 1. baptizing with the Holy Spirit and with fire (the same or two separate baptisms) and 2. Dividing or separating the wheat from the chaff seems to represent the lost from the saved.[67] A matter we will deal with for later discussion. The point to be made here is the coming of the Holy Spirit will bring a separation or a division. While there is a pouring out of God's Spirit at Pentecost and He does flow out of indwelt believers, it may also refer to an end-times release of God's Spirit before the coming of Jesus Christ to the earth-a great, Great Awakening. This end-time

---

67 This seems to support the idea of baptism with the Holy Spirit as the initial conversion experience because of the separating of the wheat from chaff. However, if there is an additional baptism of fire this could allude to the experience at Pentecost where tongues of fire appeared over the heads of those speaking in tongues. Because this is a more extended argument, I well address this matter in more detail in the next chapter.

awakening has precursors with previous revivals/ awakenings in history, all of which involved the moving of the Holy Spirit with attendant conversions and spiritual phenomena, if not miracles and healing. By now, I am assuming that you are beginning to see how this analogy is being developed. If you are not convinced then I refer you to the caution that Jesus gave to his disciples. He states, "[6] 'Be careful,' Jesus said to them. 'Be on your guard against the yeast of the Pharisees and Sadducees.' . . . [11] How is it you don't understand that I was not talking to you about bread? But be on your guard against the yeast of the Pharisees and Sadducees." [12] Then they understood that he was not telling them to guard against the yeast used in bread, but against the teaching of the Pharisees and Sadducees." First of all, yeast or leaven is typically viewed as a corrupting influence in Jewish religious understanding. The Feast of Unleavened Bread, which is a part of Passover, required the removal of all leaven/yeast from the house. This action symbolizes the removal of sin or that which is unholy. Paul uses this concept to warn the Corinthian church not to put up with sexual immorality because "a little yeast leavens the whole batch of dough?.[68]

---

68 It is actually reported that there is sexual immorality among you, and of a kind that even pagans do not tolerate:

A Most Delicate and Disturbing Matter

He suggests assenting to the erroneous actions of a few people can affect everybody. Consequently, ideas (doctrines), also, have consequences. We know this because Jesus specifically warns against the yeast of the Pharisees and the Sadducees. We are told this yeast represents their teachings. Well, what are the teachings of the Pharisees and the Sadducees? While the Pharisees did believe in miracles, angels, demons, and the resurrection, they saw these events only within the context of the past deeds of God or occurring within the confines of their understanding of how they would occur. The Pharisees represent the conservative, Reformed tradition (scripture only) or possibly fundamentalist Cessationists. On the other hand, the Sadducees denied the resurrection, angels, miracles, and other supernatural phenomena. They would represent the more liberal elements of

---

A man is sleeping with his father's wife. [2] And you are proud! Shouldn't you rather have gone into mourning and have put out of your fellowship the man who has been doing this? . . . [6] Your boasting is not good. Don't you know that a little yeast leavens the whole batch of dough? [7] Get rid of the old yeast, so that you may be a new unleavened batch—as you really are. For Christ, our Passover lamb, has been sacrificed. [8] Therefore let us keep the Festival, not with the old bread leavened with malice and wickedness, but with the unleavened bread of sincerity and truth.

190

Christian religion. The point is simple. Both groups
minimize the supernatural, particularly in association
with Jesus, who challenged their status quo and their
role in society. Jesus does not want his disciples to
"buy into" the "blindness" of either groups' teaching.
In Matthew 15:12-14, it states:

> [12] Then the disciples came to him and asked,
> "Do you know that the Pharisees
> were offended when they heard this?" [13] He
> [Jesus] replied, "Every plant that my
> heavenly Father has not planted will be
> pulled up by the roots. [14] *Leave them; they
> are blind guides* [my emphasis]. If the blind
> lead the blind, both will fall into a pit."

The very works of Jesus (miracles, healings, casting
out of demons, resurrecting people) refuted the
Sadducees, but the teaching of the Pharisees was more
pernicious because they believed in the supernatural,
but they wanted to say who was authorized to do the
supernatural. They also wanted to pontificate, about
in what "spirit" were the miracles done. At the heart
of their system of RELIGON is the reliance on human
effort instead of the Holy Spirit.[69] This yeast of self-

---

69 Galatians 5:6-9 - [6] For in Christ Jesus neither circumcision
nor uncircumcision has any value. The only thing that

reliance in one's own human effort to please God is contrary to the cross and the grace that comes by way of the Holy Spirit. The Pharisees attributed the miraculous works of Jesus to Satan. The miracles of Moses they believed in, but that had happened long ago and miracles had "ceased" for them during the inter-testamental period of scripture. To some extent, this senario is represented by Cessationism.

Cessationism is represented in some statement of faiths such as the one found in the Statement of Faith of Calvary Bible College and Seminary. Item five states, "We believe that the gift of speaking in tongues, which was a sign to the nation of Israel, and the other sign gifts gradually ceased as

---

counts is faith expressing itself through love. [7] You were running a good race. Who cut in on you to keep you from obeying the truth? [8] That kind of persuasion does not come from the one who calls you. [9] "A little yeast works through the whole batch of dough." Here, Paul is referring to obeying a religious code in order to be righteous before God. Gal. 3:1-3, [1]You foolish Galatians! Who has bewitched you? Before your very eyes Jesus Christ was clearly portrayed as crucified. [2] I would like to learn just one thing from you: Did you receive the Spirit by the works of the law, or by believing what you heard? [3] Are you so foolish? After beginning by means of the Spirit, are you now trying to finish by means of the flesh?[my emphasis].

the New Testament was completed and its authority was established (1 Cor. 13:8; 14:21-22; 2 Cor. 12:12; Heb 2:4).

One of the problems that Cessationists have is the tendency to "proof-text, i.e., simply to find scriptures that seem to support the position they are advocating regardless of context or the whole counsel of scripture. Proof-texting is considered poor hermeneutics (the science of interpretation) or "not correctly handling the word of truth (2 Timothy 2:15b).[70] How can you adamantly defend the bible while at the same time use it simply as a tool to make your case. Failure to correctly handle the scriptures dishonors the bible; it doesn't show respect for the scripture. An example of this are the four proof texts used to support Cessationism at this Bible college.

The first commonly used proof-text that has been roundly discredited, but is still used, is 1 Corinthians 13:8-9, which states, "[8] Love never fails. But where there are prophecies, they will cease; where there are tongues, they will be stilled;

---

70 2 Timothy 2:15 states, "[15] Do your best to present yourself to God as one approved, a worker who does not need to be ashamed and who correctly handles the word of truth."

where there is knowledge, it will pass away. [9] For we know in part and we prophesy in part,[10] but when completeness comes, what is in part disappears." The core of the assertion here is what disappears and when it does disappear. Cessationists maintain that tongues (and signs and wonders, which are not specifically mentioned in the text) disappeared when the perfect (KJV) or completeness comes. The critical interpretation involves knowing what the perfect or completeness represents and when did/does it come. Cessationists maintain that the perfect/ complete means with the coming together of the canon or the scriptures (New Testament specifically). There are several problems with this view.

First, the development of the canon was a process over time. The selection of when the canon was complete is an arbitrary one with scholars favoring A.D. 325 at the Council of Constantinople. This would, of course, permit tongues and miracles to extend beyond the first century and would be unacceptable to Cessationists. So, one would assume that their choice is the writing of the book of Revelation around A.D. 98 or 99. However, it is just as likely, if not more so, that the perfection or completeness that comes is a reference to Jesus at his second coming, which makes more sense given the context. Jesus is called perfect in Hebrews 2:10b

194

when it states he was made perfect (complete) by what he suffered. To suggest that the bible is more perfect or complete than Jesus is to dishonor Jesus and engage in a form of bibliolatry. The bible was inspired through human agency, which has all the additives of human personality. Doubtless, Cessationists, in their understanding of the theory of inspiration would opt toward a mechanical dictation theory, or something close to it, to preclude any idea that human agency had any effect on the scripture. However, even Paul himself at one point told the Corinthian church that what he was telling them was "not from the Lord" but was his advice to them. Jude quotes the Book of Enoch. Is this book considered just as divinely inspired? Furthermore, what about all the different human interpretations regarding the scripture? Unless you are using the bible as some kind of totem (like in Free-masonry), the point of having the bible is to apply it to life. This cannot be perfectly done if there are so many variations of interpretation. I suppose, this is why the more fundamentalist types are so adamant that they are doctrinally correct and everyone else is wrong. I understand this psychological necessity, even if it does lack humility and promotes a kind of arrogance/ pride that the scripture itself warns against. Because of the direction I took, it is probably necessary to state

195

that I believe the scriptures (original autographs) are infallible. But interpretation must be led by the author of the scripture—the Holy Spirit—using good hermeneutical practices, common sense, and higher critical thinking skills. Clearly, given the purpose of God to conform us to the image of Christ (Romans 8:29), the perfect or completeness of God is Jesus, and we will be made perfect and complete at his return.

Second, the context of the passage that suggests tongues were done away at the "coming of the canon" suffers from other elements in the passage. "But where there are prophecies, they will cease; . . . where there is knowledge, it will pass away. [9] For we know in part and we prophesy in part." Using the interpretation of Cessationists, that means that not only did tongues cease at the coming of the canon, but prophecy and knowledge also ceased. Some evangelicals interpret prophecy as "fore-telling," which they say is the act of preaching. So does preaching cease after the canon is formed? If prophecy is considered to be someone receiving divine revelation for specific matters of concern, then it is linked to tongues as a gift of the Spirit. While I am okay with that, it is not the position of some Evangelicals. But here is the big problem: how is it that knowledge ceased when the canon of scripture became fixed? When Jesus returns we are told that we will know as we are know (by Christ is inferred) because we will be like Him (made complete or perfect like Him is implied)(1 John 3:2-3).[71] This passes the common sense and good interpretation test.

Third, you cannot build an entire doctrine on a disputable passage of scripture. This is one of the basic principles of hermeneutics. Hermeneutics or the interpretation of scripture is foundational to any institution that calls itself a "bible college." A failure in the application of basic hermeneutical principles calls into question the level of scholarship and commitment one claims to have regarding respect for the scripture.   It is now time to move on to the other proof texts of this position.

Cessationists use 1 Cor. 14:21-22 to limit the use of tongues only as a sign to the people of Israel. This passage states, [21] In the Law it is written:

---

71 [2] Dear friends, now we are children of God, and what we will be has not yet been made known. But we know that when Christ appears, we shall be like him, for we shall see him as he is. [3] All who have this hope in him purify themselves, just as he is pure.

> With other tongues and through the lips
> of foreigners I will speak to this people,
> but even then they will not listen to me,
> says the Lord. [22] Tongues, then, are a sign,
> not for believers but for unbelievers;
> prophecy, however, is not for unbelievers
> but for believers.

Cessationists want to limit the role of tongues simply as a "sign" that was given to the Jews in order to convince them of the authenticity of the mission of Jesus Christ as the Messiah (even though Jesus himself never spoke in a public tongue as recorded in the gospels).[72] However, tongues in the context of the church at Corinth, was used to convince unbelieving *gentiles* of the authenticity of the Christian faith. Here, Paul is not referring to Jews at all. Apparently, in this context, tongues are valid and important to convince the lost. I think we still encounter lost people even today. In fairness, (something the Cessationist proof-texting avoids), tongues were a sign to the Corinthian non-Christians

---

72 If tongues validated the ministry of Jesus to the Jews, then why isn't it recorded in scripture that Jesus spoke in tongues? If applied only to believers after Jesus ascension, how is tongues connected with the gospel of Christ if he never spoke in togues?

because they recognized "ecstatic" utterance as a sign of "a god" speaking through an adherent of a pagan faith. So, Paul suggests tongues serves a purpose, in this regard, of reaching this gentile population that valued ecstatic utterance (tongues). This has led some to suggest that tongues were confronted by Paul because it was a pagan practice that entered the church (a position gleefully accepted by some Cessationists). However, this is false because Paul says he speaks in tongues more than any of them and tells them not to forbid its exercise in the church (see the chapter on tongues). So in a sense tongues is a "sign" to unbelievers within the cultural context of people groups that are non-western in their worldview, i.e., believe in the everyday reality of the supernatural. In a narrow or limited sense, something I am not sure Cessationists want to acknowledge, tongues is best exercised in non-western nations. This means, happily for Evangelicals, tongues is more accepted and has more of a "sign" function outside of the United States and Europe. However, there is a down side. The culture of the bible is Middle Eastern, not American or European. An inability to understand that culture impoverishes our understanding of the bible and leads us to unwarranted conclusions about the scriptures.[73]

Additionally, Cessationists want to assert that only apostles do "signs and wonders, but according to the scriptures this is incorrect. They use 2 Corinthians 12:12 which states, "[12] I persevered in demonstrating among you the marks of a true apostle, including signs, wonders and miracles." However, this is incorrect. While the marks of a true apostle are "signs, wonders and miracles," apostles were not the only individuals who did signs and wonders. If you claim that the apostles were the twelve, with the possible inclusion of Paul (maybe Barnabus and Silas), then when the original

---

73 For example, when the scripture says it rains on the just and unjust alike, it is not referring to problems that come upon believers and non-believers (as in don't rain on my parade). Understanding the importance of rain in the Middle East changes the perspective of the interpretation. Rain is a blessing in a desert climate. So, interpreted correctly, God blesses the just and the unjust. Likewise, "heaping coals on someone's head" doesn't make sense if you respond in kindness toward someone who abuses you. It is not God's desire for you to be kind in order to make someone feel bad. In the Middle East, bundles were carried on top of the head. In this case, coals are a good thing because they are used to cook food and heat a home. This is an example of Hebrew parallelism. Kind words are like giving someone something they really need.

individuals who walked with Jesus on the earth died out then it is assumed that signs and wonders died out. This understanding is incorrect for a few reasons. First, the New Testament, clearly, identifies people who were not "apostles" in the restricted sense of the term. Luke 9:1-2 states, "And he called the twelve and gave them power and authority over all demons and to cure diseases and he sent them out to proclaim the kingdom of God and to heal." Notice, preaching and healing was done at the same time. However, more importantly, in Luke 10:1, 9, 17 we see that Jesus sent out 72 others to do the same things that he sent out the twelve to do. Luke 10:1,9, and 17 states, "After this the Lord appointed seventy-two others and sent them ahead of him . . . . Heal the sick in it [town] and say the kingdom of God has come near you . . . . The seventy-two returned with joy saying, 'Lord, even the demons are subject to us in your name.'" Signs and wonders were done by Philip, the deacon turned evangelist. In Acts 8:5-8, we are told, "Philip went down to the city of Samaria and proclaimed to them the Christ Philip went down the city of Samaria and proclaimed to them the Christ. And the crowds with one accord paid attention to what was being said by Philip when they heard him saw the signs that he did. For unclean spirits, crying out with a loud voice, came out of many who had

201

them, and many who were paralyzed or lame were healed. So there was much joy in that city. " Later on in the chapter, it states, "and seeing signs and great miracles performed, he [Simon] was amazed" (Acts 8:13b).   Agabus, a prophet, exercised revelational gifts without being an apostle. Furthermore, it is not true that the ministry of the apostle ended after the first century. First of all, there were apostles beyond the twelve disciples, and the book of James, Mark (although seen as a secretary to Peter in regard to the gospel), Luke, and the book of Acts were not written by apostles. Yet, these books of the bible are heralded by those who want to suggest a special status to the apostles that no longer exists today. There were and are apostles that existed outside of the twelve then and are still with us today.   In Ephesians 4:11-15 it sates,

> [11] So Christ himself gave the apostles, the prophets, the evangelists, the pastors and teachers, [12] to equip his people for works of service, so that the body of Christ may be built up[13] until we all reach unity in the faith and in the knowledge of the Son of God and become mature, attaining to the whole measure of the fullness of Christ. [14] Then we will no longer be infants, tossed back and forth by the waves, and blown here

and there by every wind of teaching and by the cunning and craftiness of people in their deceitful scheming.[15] Instead, speaking the truth in love, we will grow to become in every respect the mature body of him who is the head, that is, Christ.

The duration for the existence of these five ministries (four if you combine pastor and teacher) are "until we all reach unity in the faith and in the knowledge of the Son of God and become mature, attaining to the whole measure of the fullness of Christ." This has not happened yet. Furthermore, the ministry of these individuals is to equip his people for works of service. There is an ongoing ministry to be performed by apostles and prophets. The evangelist, pastor and teacher did not disappear after the first century, but neither did the apostle and the prophet. All the ministries are needed until believers are thoroughly equipped for works of service and until they attain the whole measure of the fullness of Christ. The refusal to recognize any of these ministries as active in equipping today means that the congregation will not receive the benefits of those ministries. So if the apostle is still around even today that means signs and wonders are around today. However, even if that is not true, it is not necessary for there to be an apostle, in the strictest sense (according to

Cessationists), because Jesus has specifically said that any believer can perform the miracles that he performed. Jesus said,

> [10] Don't you believe that I am in the Father, and that the Father is in me? The words I say to you I do not speak on my own authority. Rather, it is the Father, living in me, who is doing his work. [11] Believe me when I say that I am in the Father and the Father is in me; or at least believe on the evidence of the works themselves. [12] Very truly I tell you, *whoever believes in me will do the works I have been doing* [my emphasis], and they will do even greater things than these, because I am going to the Father. [13] And I will do whatever you ask in my name, so that the Father may be glorified in the Son. [14] You may ask me for anything in my name, and I will do it

Jesus begins by telling his disciples that the miracles that he does do not proceed out of his God nature, but, instead, proceeds out of his anointed human nature it is the Father in him who is doing the works. From the context, we understand that the word

works means miracles.[74]   Even though Jesus tells

---

74 The actual Greek word for works is whatever a person does. So a farmer is engaged in farming and a teacher is involved in teaching. However, the context suggests that which would convince a person of the legitimacy of Jesus's claim to be the Messiah and being the image of the Father. The same word that is used for works in this passage is also found in John the third chapter where Nicodemus tells Jesus that "no man can if do the things that you are doing if God were not with him." Additionally, in Acts 10:38 we read, "Jesus went about doing good healing all that were oppressed by the devil." Furthermore, I was told in seminary that the greater works was the ability to preach the gospel using the radio, television, print etc. Greek Scholar A.T. Robertson in examining the word "works" within its grammatical context notes that the word can mean "greater in number" or "greater in kind" (or both). My professor chose to use "greater in number" but then also limited the activities of Jesus in his earthly ministry only to preaching. This does not reflect the context of the passage, which deals with confirming Jesus' supernatural ministry as the messiah. Also, the choice of disregarding the translation of the term "greater works" as "greater in kind" is an interpretive move designed to make the scriptures conform to one's own opinion. This is called eisogesis (reading into the text) and is discouraged as a hermeneutical practice. They wanted me to believe that the greater works were not tied specifically to the kind of ministry Jesus did, but simply a greater ministry because there were more gospel preachers in the earth,

Philip that the works testify that He and the Father are one, Jesus goes on to say "whoever believes in me will do the works I have been doing." Jesus does not limit this to his twelve disciples alone. The word whoever is the same word that is used in John 3:16, For God so loved the world that he gave his one and only Son, that **whoever** *believes in him* [my emphasis] shall not perish but have eternal life. If you believe that salvation is available to whoever believes, then you have to believe that the doing of miracles is available to whoever believes.

Cessationists want to tie signs and wonders only to the confirmation of the veracity of the gospel, suggesting that they are not important in and of themselves. Some use this scripture passage to make this point: Heb 2:3b-4 states, "This salvation, which was first announced by the Lord, was confirmed to us by those who heard him.[4] God also testified to it [salvation] by signs, wonders and various miracles, and by gifts of the Holy Spirit distributed

---

while there was only one Jesus. This is NOT in keeping with the context. To ignore the supernatural ministry of believers is an ideological choice not in keeping with the scripture passage. Such an opinion then is not biblical, but a misreading of the text.

according to his will." The writer of the Book of Hebrews states that the gospel was confirmed to him and others by those who actually heard Jesus speak of salvation. Additionally, this salvation was also confirmed by "signs, wonders and various miracles, and by gifts of the Holy Spirit." Cessationists want to tie signs and wonders only to the salvation that was originally announced by Jesus. However, the gifts of the Holy Spirit, distributed according to his will, are still being distributed even today. Paul makes that very clear in First Corinthians. If the gifts are still for today, then signs and wonders are still for today.

Now comes the test of logic which is used to validate or invalidate arguments. If we use a logical (categorical) syllogism, the argument of Cessationism can be viewed this way:

> Premise 1: All miracles done by God ceased by the end of the first century.
>
> Premise 2: Any miracles done apart from God are demonic
>
> Conclusion: Miracles done today are demonic because God's miracles ceased at the end of the first century.

This syllogism is only valid if all the premises are true. Clearly, the second premise is acceptable. The first premise, however, is what is in dispute. If the first premise is not accepted, then the syllogism fails or is invalid. In fact, it is the first premise that is contested or must be proven. This is an example of the logical fallacy of "circular reasoning" or "begging the question". Additionally, the only thing that is necessary to invalidate the first premise is to prove that a miracle took place after the first century. Because the first premise is an absolute statement, it only requires one exception to invalidate it. Church history is full of examples of miracles having taken place among various denominations and, even today, there are verified and recorded miracles in this country and other countries around the world. So, let's begin to refute Cessationism starting with the Patristic Period (A.D. 100-600), which is clearly after the death of the original apostles. Justin Martyr in his *Second Apology* (circa 153) writes, "For numberless demoniacs throughout the whole world, and in your city, many of our Christian men exorcising them in the name of Jesus Christ, who was crucified under Pontius Pilate, have healed and do deal, rendering helpless and driving the possessing devils out of the men, though they could not be cured by all the other exorcists, and those who use incantations and drugs" (qtd. by Wimber 210). Irenaeus, the Bishop of Lyons, states: "For some do certainly and truly drive out Devils, so that those who have thus been cleansed from evil spirits frequently join themselves the church. Others have foreknowledge of things to come: they see visions, and other prophetic expressions. Other still, heal the sick by laying their hands upon them, and they are made whole, Yea, moreover, as I have said, the dead even have been raised up, and remained among us for many years" (Irenaeus, *Against Heresies* qtd. by Wimber 211). By the fourth century, Novation of Rome, in chapter 29 of his *Treatise Concerning the Trinity* states, "this is He [Holy Spirit] who places prophets in the church, instructs teachers, directs tongues, gives powers and healings, does wonderful works, offers discrimination of spirits, affords powers of government, suggests counsels, and orders and arranges whatever other gifts there are of *charismata*" (qtd. by Wimber 212). I will close out the end of the third century by mentioning Augustine who wrote *The City of God* (circa 413-427). Augustine records at least 19 varieties of supernatural events including the healing of sight, gout, breast cancer, rectal fistula, paralysis, and a hernia. He also speaks about a resurrection from the dead and two instances where demons were cast out of individuals. I will skip the medieval period since it is basically a recorded history primarily related to the Catholic Church (generally mistrusted by evangelicals who are suspicious of the "extra biblical", "superstitious" tendencies denomination).[75]

The period of the Reformation, however, should be close to the heart of most Evangelicals. Martin Luther in one of his letters gives a procedure to deal with melancholy that is caused by the devil saying, "graciously deign to free this man from all evil, and put to not the work that Satan has done to him . . . . Then when you depart, lay your hands upon the man again and say, 'these signs shall follow them that believe; they shall lay hands on the sick, and they will recover'" (Wimber 223). Another reformer, John Wesley, founder of the Methodist Church, wrote in his *Journal*, "I was fully convinced of what I had once suspected: (1) that the Montanists, in the second and third centuries, were real, scriptural Christians; and (2) That the grand reason why the miraculous gifts were so soon withdrawn, was not only that faith and holiness were wellnigh [*sic*] lost, but that dry, formal, orthodox men began even then to ridicule whatever gifts they had not themselves, and to decry them all as either madness or imposture" (Wimber

---

75 I, personally, do not mistrust these accounts, but I would rather not use examples that would be rejected out of hand by some. Remember, only one post-apostolic example is necessary to refute Cessationism.

228-229). Additionally, Wesley wrote in a letter to Thomas Church in June 1746 the following: "Yet I do not know that God hath anyway precluded himself from thus exerting His sovereign power from working miracles in any kind or degree in any age to the end of the world. I do not recollect any scripture wherein the limits of the apostolic or the Cyprianic age, or of any period of time, longer or shorter, even till the restitution of all things. I have not observed, either in the Old Testament, or the New, any intimation at all of this kind" (Wimber 229). Here we see John Wesley, founder of the Methodist church, asserting that miracles were possible even during his day. How closely does the Methodist Church give consideration to Wesley's remarks? Wesley was not a Cessationist.

I will dispense with the accounting of the miracles recorded by innumerable ministries and ministers from Pentecostals, the healing revivalists of the 1950s (William Branham, Oral Roberts, T.L. Osborn), and international evangelists and missionaries such as Charles Finney, J.G. Lake, Reinhard Bonnke, and Heidi Baker, since these ministries are not as convincing to some Evangelicals. Baker has witnessed many healings and miracles, including at least ten resurrections, and a miracle of increase.

The doctrine: "All miracles done by God

211

ceased by the end of the first century," fails the test of logic and fails when you apply "the correspondence theory of truth."[76]   More importantly, I can attest to several healings that have taken place in my ministry and those associated with me including a deaf person who was healed, a Downs syndrome baby was healed, and a woman with cancer was healed. Additionally, since 1986 I have been involved in casting out demons from over 350 to 400 people. I can never be convinced that the supernatural ministry of the Holy Spirit ceased two thousand years ago. I would have to stifle a laugh if someone tried to convince me that was true. In short, this doctrine is bogus.

Up to now we have dealt with delicate matters, but now it is time to deal with a potentially disturbing matter—the relationship of doctrines to demons. 1 Timothy 4:1 states, "The Spirit clearly says that in later times some will abandon the faith and follow deceiving spirits and *things taught by demons*

---

76 This test for truth maintains that for an assertion to be true, it must be true regarding the reality found in the natural realm. That means when you see a comet, if you can observe it is a comet and not a visible to the naked eye angel falling from heaven, then it is a comet. It corresponds to reality.

[my emphasis]." First of all, there is a suggestion that following deceiving spirits and things taught by demons result in the abandoning of the faith (once for all delivered as Paul would say). Clearly, we can see this in the proliferation of cults claiming to be sects of Christianity, yet denying essential orthodox doctrines about Christ. These groups are not Christian: Mormons, Jehovah Witnesses, Unity, etc. because they deny that Jesus Christ is God come in the flesh. The apostle John says in First John that the denial of Jesus having come in the flesh is a doctrine of the spirit of antichrist. Thus, as Cessationists would agree, there are deceiving spirits (demons) in the world today who promote heresy that lead to an abandoning of the faith. In fact, Paul says that all false religion is influenced or energized by demons. However, this passage specifically deals with those who deny the Trinity or the deity of Christ (other religions, as well) who were once "Christian" but not really (they went out from us because they were never a part of us, John says). Now here is the part that gets disturbing.

I believe there are doctrines taught or used by demons to make Christians ineffective, guilt ridden, and divisive or even hateful toward other Christians. Some of these doctrines have a "spirit" to them. For example, when the sons of thunder (James

213

and John) wanted to call down fire from heaven to burn up the Samaritans for not receiving Jesus, Jesus said to them "you do not know what spirit you are of" (Luke 9:55 KJV).[77] Jesus implies that there is a "spirit" behind what the disciples wanted to do. It was not the same spirit that he had, but a different spirit. Jesus told his disciples that his words were Spirit and life. In John 6:63 Jesus states, "[63] The Spirit gives life; the flesh counts for nothing. The words I have spoken to you—they are full of the Spirit and life." In short, there are spiritual forces at work using the words spoken or ideas conveyed in order to serve their interests. The Holy Spirit serves the interests of God and demons serve the interests of Satan.

Previously, I discussed the doctrine that all miracles done by God ceased by the end of the first century and, therefore, miracles done today are demonic. This has led some evangelicals, in general,

---

77 The text states: "[52] And sent messengers before his face: and they went, and entered into a village of the Samaritans, to make ready for him. [53] And they did not receive him, because his face was as though he would go to Jerusalem. [54] And when his disciples James and John saw this, they said, Lord, wilt thou that we command fire to come down from heaven, and consume them, even as Elias did? [55] But he turned, and rebuked them, and said, Ye know not what manner of spirit ye are of (Luke 9:52-55).

and Cessationists, in particular, to claim that "tongues are of the devil" or that the miracles done in the last days are designed to deceive believers so that they will abandon the faith. However, those Christians, who exercise tongues and are seeing miracles in their life and ministry, are not abandoning the faith. In fact, they are finding their love for Jesus increased and are actively involved in advancing the kingdom of God and his Christ. Is it possible that an over emphasis on the supernatural could lead to a distraction from the agenda of the kingdom and, also, lead to pride? Well, yes. Is it possible that a rejection of the supernatural could stymie the agenda of the Kingdom of God and lead to doctrinal pride and a divisive and unloving attitude toward other Christians? Well, yes. The point is human beings can always be tempted to live in the flesh. But what seems to be the likely agenda of demons: "a form of godliness denying the power" (Cessationism) or "twisting the desire to see God express himself in the earth through believers through counterfeit expressions of miracles to entice Christians away from God?" First of all, the Cessationist position is untenable. Second, if there is a counterfeit, there is a real. Third, why is it that demons are more powerful in the earth than Jesus/ the Holy Spirit (Greater is He that is in you than he that is in the world). Fourth, why would Christians

215

A Most Delicate and Disturbing Matter

support a view that essentially makes God mute (doesn't speak today), impotent (doesn't intervene miraculously), and gives more glory to the devil and his deeds. Finally, it makes more sense that demons would twist the meaning of scripture to make believers less of a threat to them and their work (the casting out of demons is a supernatural work that is going on today that confronts demons where they live).[78] Cessationism is based on one basic fact: the person who holds this view has not experienced the obvious manifestation of the supernatural in his or her own life. They don't trust experience (see earlier chapter) and they surround themselves with like-minded people/teachers who re-enforce this doctrine to the exclusion of other possibilities.[79]

---

78 Since 1986, I have ministered to hundreds of people casting out multiple demons from individuals who were oppressed.

79 2 Timothy 4:3 states, "[3] For the time will come when people will not put up with sound doctrine. Instead, to suit their own desires, they will gather around them a great number of teachers to say what their itching ears want to hear. [4] They will turn their ears away from the truth and turn aside to myths." The myth of the cessation of miracles has been established earlier. Why is this often repeated maxim still prevalent among some evangelicals? Perhaps it is time to separate the commentary notes of C.I.

216

In short, I believe that Cessationism is a doctrine taught by demons and energized by a pharisaical spirit of division, "a zeal not according to knowledge" (Rom. 10:2). But cessationism is not the only doctrine that is taught by or of demons.

C.S. Lewis said the greatest lie the devil ever perpetrated on humanity is that he did not exist. I would add that the second greatest lie is that Christians are somehow immune from demonic influence or oppression. Certain doctrines or beliefs are reinforced by feelings that are energized by demonic activity sometimes based on negative experiences one has had with any particular group. One of the basic fears one may face is the fear of the unknown, the loss of control or to place "one's ministry career" in jeopardy to pursue the truth. There is a demon that reinforces fear and it can influence Christians. Covetousness or jealousy is also an emotion along with selfish ambition, where you find every evil practice (James 3:16-- For where you have envy and **selfish ambition**, there you find disorder and every evil practice). The entire discussion

---

Scofield from the actual inspired text of the bible. There has been some confusion at the point of accepting a man's interpretive opinion as the legitimate and only position on the scripture.

of Ephesians 6:10-12 reminds the Christian that we are in a struggle or a war, and where there is a war there are casualties.[80]

No discussion about the influence of demons on Christian behavior would be complete without addressing the pharisaical tendency toward heresy hunting. There is a difference between pastoral concern for one's own parishioners and, even if you grant that there are Christian "statesmen" who are respected enough to speak to the entire body of Christ, and those who are involved in character assassination, deceptive evaluation, and "bad faith" or a spirit bolstered by pride and judgmentalism. The Pharisees were the heresy hunters who attacked Jesus, the living word of God and the complete revelation of the Father (Hebrew 1:1-2). Jesus called them prideful (wanting fame), greedy, hypocritical, and slanderous. They called Jesus a glutton and a drunkard, a spawn of Satan, a sinner, a false Messiah, and a law breaker (character assassination). The

---

80 "Finally, be strong in the Lord and in his mighty power. [11] Put on the full armour of God, so that you can take your stand against the devil's schemes. [12] For our struggle is not against flesh and blood, but against the rulers, against the authorities, against the powers of this dark world and against the spiritual forces of evil in the heavenly realms."

Pharisees constantly subjected Jesus to cross-examination throughout his ministry and eventually put him on trial and sentenced him to death. Fast forward to the Middle Ages and you will find the Catholic Inquisition burning heretics at the stake (after bringing the heretic to trial of course). Hunting heretics, however, did not end with the Catholic church and the Inquisition. Reformation hero Martin Luther persecuted the radical reformation Anabaptists; John Calvin (original Calvinist) burned Savanarola at the stake in Genoa for being a heretic. The Puritans (good Calvinists), England's dissenters from the state sponsored Anglican church, in turn, executed eighteen people accused of being witches during the Salem Witch Trials (giving rise to the despicable term 'witch hunt').

In the modern era there have been several individuals concerned about the "corruption" of Christianity and organizations who are "watch dogs" regarding "Christian" Cults. These cult watching organizations have served a good apologetic service to the body of Christ in dealing with cults, but have strayed into attacking certain revival movements. As an apologetics teacher, I appreciate and use the book *Kingdom of the Cults* (I own three of its various revisions including editors Walter Martin, Hank Hanegraaff, and Ravi Zacharias). The Christian

Research Institute, the publisher of these books, the *Christian research Journal*, and the program *The Bible Answer Man*, began to become more critical of Holy Spirit based organizations after the death of Walter Martin and the assumption of leadership by Hank Hanegraaff. Today, Hanegraaff is the director of CRI and is the Bible Answer Man and has written a book entitled *Christianity in Crisis* a work that is highly critical of the Word of Faith movement. Additionally, Hanegraaff is critical of the "Laughing" revival apparently based mostly on his own personal preference for a more reverent decorum. Hanegraaff, who originally described himself as a Charismatic, now, distances himself from the movement.

Perhaps it is time to put into practice what the scriptures have to say regarding some of the tactics of heresy hunters. When you take quotes out of context or use the "strawman" logical fallacy[81] you

81 The Strawman fallacy is when an opponent takes the most objectionable examples of a person's opinion or behavior and suggests that the entire movement, entity, or person is represented by those examples. In essence, it is "constructing" an enemy based on an unfair and untruthful representation. Atheists declare that Christianity (religion) has done more harm in the world than any other ideology (which is false, atheistic Nazis killed at least 6 million people, Stalin's atheistic communism killed over 10

are involved in deception (distortion and half truths are considered lies). Hanegraaff is involved in this practice in pulling out of context some of the most objectionable quotes and then building "a case"[82] (straight from the playbook of the Inquisition and common in both the legal and political processes of the United States) against the Word of Faith Movement. Also, not everyone who is a part of the Word of Faith movement holds the same opinions, although there seems to be some core understandings.[83] Hanegraaff

---

million) citing the Crusades and the Spanish Inquisition. This common assertion by atheists and Bill Mahr ignores all the philanthropic work Christianity has been engaged in. Thus, it is a Strawman argument that is deceptive and illogical (a logical fallacy). Atheists who pride themselves on being so smart (Richard Dawkins likes to call atheists "Brights") are committing a logical fallacy, i.e., using poor critical thinking skills.

82 The early church fathers wrote against heretical movements, but they did so from a pastoral corrective position. They wanted to redeem or save people from deception. This began to change when the church considered doctrine more important than people. Paul said we should "speak the truth IN LOVE [my emphasis]" (Eph. 4:15).

83 I, personally, am not a fan of the Word of Faith message. I am not interested in calling it a heresy; although, I disagree

is not the only heresy hunter worthy of mention.

Prior to Hanegraaff's book, Dave Hunt wrote *The Seduction of Christianity* in which he used the tactic of "guilt by association" (this involves the "slippery slope" fallacy, "poisoning the well" fallacy, "post hoc" fallacy and, more precisely, the "genetic" fallacy).[84]   What does James Dobson (evangelical),

---

with some of the core understanding and applications of the theology. Ideas have consequences and it is some of those consequences that I want to avoid. To me, Dispensationalism is more of a heresy than this movement, but since it is a part of evangelical consensus theology it is unlikely to be deemed a heresy, especially since that is the economic base of CRI (this latter comment is unfair, because it attributes a motive to CRI that is not proven. Furthermore, it is an example of the ad hominum ("to the man"; an assault on the character of an opponent) logical fallacy because I suggested that money plays a role in whom they criticize. This reduces their ethos and impugns, in a subtle way, their reputation. So, I retract it. I simply use this statement to show how easy it is to be unfair).

84 The "slippery slope" fallacy suggests that if you accept one erroneous position then it opens the door to additional erroneous positions leading to catastrophe (e.g., teenage holding hands leads to pre-marital sex); "poisoning the well" fallacy suggests that an unfavorable aspect of a person or his or her opinion means that all

John Wimber (reformed Charismatic), Robert Schuler (positive thinking preacher, who wrote the concordance for Calvin's *Institutes of Religion*), Agnes Sanford (early proponent of inner healing or the healing of memories) all have in common? They are involved in seducing Christians and perverting "pure" Christianity. Hunt links these people together because, at one time or another, each one had a "connection" or made a favorable mention of the others. Hunt, who is anti-psychology and hence anti-Christian psychology, "traces" the influence of "new age' movement and theosophy on Sanford condemning her and then everyone that had any association or opinion that appeared to be similar to Sanford (Poison the Well fallacy). His objection to all

teaching associated with the person is suspect (e.g., if there is just one mistake in the bible you cannot trust any of it); Post Hoc fallacy suggests that similar views came from each other (comparable bone structures in animals means that creatures evolved or came from each other); and, more precisely, the Genetic fallacy suggests that a position ought to be rejected because a proponent of the position was associated with someone who is in error or is not trustworthy (e.g., Heidi Baker went to Toronto during the "Father's Blessing revival and received a touch from God. However, the extreme manifestations, including animal noises, are extra-biblical and therefore Baker cannot be trusted, by association).

223

kinds of psychology is based on the idea of reinforcing "self esteem" instead of realizing that people or sinners and are simply in need of the cross/gospel. I was given Hunt's book, *The Seduction of Christianity*, by a well-intentioned friend within a year after I had a dramatic life-changing experience with the Holy Spirit (I mention this experience in the preface). Even though my experience was legitimate and resulted in the character of Christ and the ability to do supernatural ministry, Hunt's unprincipled attack on John Wimber, shook my faith and momentarily caused me to doubt my experience because I was still evangelical enough and unaware of his illogical tactics. My response to what he said was not one of being convinced, but a kind of fear came over me, which I realized later was influenced by a demon. Even though I knew the truth, the emotion of fear, engendered within a certain evangelical cultural context and reinforced by a demon, was aimed at pulling me away from the truth of my experience. It is the only book I have ever read that I have thrown into the trash because of a particular message.[85] I

---

85 I have read and keep a copy of the Koran (Qur'an) and writings of other world religions. I love books. My action was based on taking a stand before God in my commitment to Him. I read materials by people who object to my belief system (a lot of times I get their books from the library

discerned it was dangerous, because it was filled with character assassination designed to hurt my relationship with Jesus. It is my understanding that John MacArthur has become one of the biggest and most well-know critics of Charismatics. Since, at the time of writing this book, I have not read his books on Charismatics, I have no comment to make regarding MacArthur. Years ago (1980s), I read his book *Body Dynamics* and even used it as a source in my doctoral project dissertation. At that time, MacArthur suggested that the church's ministry should be based on the exercise of the spiritual gifts of its members and not simply plugging people into ministry on the basis of need or talents. This impacted me in my pre-spirit-filled days. I appreciate what he said among some other things that were impactful. His current position does not invalidate the truth of his previous statements. Having given some examples of heresy hunting by some well-known individuals, I want to emphasize that, to a lesser degree, this attitude can exist among rank and file evangelicals, as well. Famous or not, the scriptures have much to say to those who would engage in heresy hunting, in terms

---

because I don't want to financially support their views, but if I want to write a response I will sometimes purchase the book).

of tone and tactics.

Charles H. Kraft in his book *Christianity with Power* does an excellent job pointing out the difference between the early apologists, who addressed heretical movements in the church and the kind of heresy hunting that is currently being practiced.[86]

---

86 Interestingly enough, the Montanists, considered by some to be the earliest Charismatic movement, were opposed by many of the early apologists, mainly because of their practices. The Montanists emphasized the immediacy of the Holy Spirit and practiced tongues and prophecy in their meetings. They also validated women in ministry at a time when the church was beginning to become more patriarchal and Catholic in its structure. I suspect the unwillingness of the Montanists to submit to the authority structure of the second century church and its predisposition to curtail female leadership may have been the primary reason for it falling into disfavour. Despite the general lack of good will toward the Montanists, they can claim one highly respected early church leader—Tertullian.   Tertullian appreciated their fervour and commitment to the Lord. Of special note, the Montanists, perhaps more than any other group at the time, embraced martyrdom for the faith (this became a problem in the early church because of the readiness of Christians to follow Jesus into a martyr's death was seen as an unwise depletion of the Christian ranks for the purpose of gaining special favour in heaven and recognition on

First of all, the basic principles of determining what should guide anyone seeking to reprove the body of Christ are found in the scripture itself. This is appropriate because it is the scripture that is being defended. A person should not be defending scripture while at the same time violating scripture. In Ephesians 4:22-30 it states,

> [22] You were taught, with regard to your former way of life, to put off your old self, which is being corrupted by its deceitful desires; [23] to be made new in the attitude of your minds; [24] and to put on the new self, created to be like God in true righteousness and holiness. [25] Therefore each of you must put off falsehood and speak truthfully to your neighbor, for we are all members of one body. [26] "In your anger do not sin": Do not let the sun go down while you are still angry, [27] and do not give the devil a foothold. . . .
>
> [29] Do not let any unwholesome talk come out of your mouths, but only what is helpful for building others up according to

earth). If the Montanist movement had been corrected, as opposed to being suppressed, it leads one to wonder what kind of Christianity would have developed.

> their needs, that it may benefit those who
> listen. [30] And do not grieve the Holy Spirit of
> God, with whom you were sealed for the day
> of redemption. [31] Get rid of all bitterness,
> rage and anger, brawling and slander, along
> with every form of malice. [32] Be kind and
> compassionate to one another, forgiving
> each other, just as in Christ God forgave you.

The context of this passage is Paul reminding the
Ephesian church that they are not to live like pagans,
obeying their deceitful desires, which is a part of the
old self (nature). Instead they are to put on the new
self, which is like God and engenders a new attitude.
Verse 25, which begins with the word "therefore,"
is a classic Pauline way of applying this admonition.
The first general principle that Paul lays down is verse
29, where he states, "[29] Do not let any unwholesome
talk come out of your mouths, but only what is
helpful for building others up according to their
needs, that it may benefit those who listen." Here we
see that the concern is placed on the hearer, which
includes not only the people who are to be "saved"
from failing into a so-called "Charismatic heresy,"
but it also includes those who are the subject of
the "correction." The motive or tone of addressing
differences of opinion is based on two things: 1. Does
it build people up or benefit those that listen? and 2.

Is the speech wholesome? Additionally, Paul takes into consideration the effect of the unwholesome talk on the speaker himself. It should be noted that one of the motives for "unwholesome talk" is "bitterness, rage and anger, brawling and slander, along with every form of malice."[87] Charismatic believers have come to believe that certain anti-Charismatic believers simply do not like them and wish them and the movement ill-will. They get this impression because of the unfair tactics that are

───────────────

87 Any discussion of speech must be founded on the fact it is a representation of the heart. Jesus sates in Matthew 15: 17-18, "But what comes out of the mouth comes from the heart, and this is what makes a man 'unclean'" or defiles him. It is not what you do on the outside-- what you bring into the body-- that defiles you. Jesus says that you defile yourself by your own mouth, that out of the abundance of the heart the mouth speaks and reveals the heart. Words are powerful. When we hear what we say we are making a confession of what is on our heart. Believing in the heart (sincerity or truthfulness) and confession that Jesus is Lord results in salvation. Believing in your heart a lie and confessing it also has power over your life. We are accountable. First, we are accountable for our words. In [Matthew 12: 36] Jesus states, "But I tell you on the day of judgement, men will have to give an account for every idle,[that is every inoperative or non-working] word they speak," they will have to give an account of that as to whether or not it was useful or useless.

used against them and the fact that it seems that some have made it their personal mission in life to oppose their belief system. For example, there are some atheists who are not zealous in their attack on God and religion, and then there are some who are hell-bent on trying to remove any influence of religion in society. These latter atheists spend more time thinking and speaking about God and religion than the nominal Christian who has been secularized and does not give any thought about God on a regular basis. Atheists that are zealous (angry) seem to be motivated either by anger or bitterness, having come to the conclusion that religion is bad or dangerous because of either a personal offense or a feeling of having been duped by religion at some point in their lives (clearly, a motive is the need to do whatever one wants in life apart from the fear of ultimate accountability, but that is beyond the text under consideration). I think, at this point, it is necessary for heresy hunters to become honest with themselves about their personal motivations: Are you angry or bitter or have malice towards those you are "correcting?" If these emotions or attitudes are a part of the crusade against Charismatic believers then you very likely will be involved in the later part of verse 31 "brawling and slander, along with every form of malice." What Paul is saying here is that anger, rage, and bitterness can lead to brawling and slander. But let's say for the moment there is not anger, rage or bitterness involved. Paul is still saying that brawling (quarreling/overly zealous debate) and slander (the attempt to damage someone's character by accusation) are things to be avoided because this gives "the devil a foothold." A foothold is not only an access point for the devil to work in a believer's life (Paul is addressing Christians here) but is a point of establishment in the believer's life. In short, apart from the love and compassion of Jesus that informs any true correction, a heresy hunter is in danger of being used by the devil to do his own work. This is a strong assertion, but it follows naturally from the very nature of Satan himself.

The word for slander in the scripture is "*diabolos*" it means ***false accusation or slander***. And it literally is translated as <u>the word for the devil</u>, the word that refers to Satan, proper. You won't find it translated "false accusations" in scripture. There is a different word for demons, so the word devil should only be singular in reference to Satan and not "devils" as in referring to demons. Satan is not only called the "Father of Lies" (which is one reason why Christians must not lie), but he is also called "the accuser (slanderer) of the brethren. **Slander** means to *accuse someone in such a way as to rob them of reputation,*

231

to injure, to malign them, to hurt them in some way with words, and to cause defamation to come upon them and question come upon their character. In every form of slander there is an accusation. Satan is an accuser of the brethren; that makes him well qualified to be a heresy hunter, at least, one who knows no compassion or love for the brethren.[88]

Furthermore, Paul had his fill of being judged and accused/slandered by the "false apostles." His attitude was not to become involved in responding to criticisms of his ministry. He states.

---

88 There is a godly way of bringing correction to the body of Christ. A person must first examine his or her own hearts to remove any plank from his or her own eye. A series of questions should be asked: 1. Is there any woundedness by Christians, churches or those representing the objects of criticism? 2. Are there doctrinal differences (liberal, fundamentalist, Arminian, calvinistic, etc) that are not essential to the unity of the Christian faith? 3. Is there an ethical perspective (pastor or church chooses luxury, not minority friendly etc) that the bible does not clearly condemn? And 4. Is there a personal preference (worship style, church polity, etc.) that is being defended apart from a clear biblical standard? Additionally, one should consider the following: 1. Do you have an attitude of superiority?; 2. Are you willing to associate with people of the group that you have differences with?; 3. Do you use "name calling," unfavourable comparisons and metaphors, or ad hominum attacks?

This, then, is how you ought to regard us: as servants of Christ and as those entrusted with the mysteries God has revealed. [2] Now it is required that those who have been given a trust must prove faithful. [3] I care very little if I am judged by you or by any human court; indeed, I do not even judge myself. [4] My conscience is clear, but that does not make me innocent. It is the Lord who judges me. [5] Therefore judge nothing before the appointed time; wait until the Lord comes. He will bring to light what is hidden in darkness and will expose the motives of the heart. At that time each will receive their praise from God. (1 Corinthians 4:1-5)

Paul goes on to state that he would confront those who were trying to subvert the churches he had established on the basis on "a sincere and pure devotion to Christ." Did he plan on arguing with them? No. Here is what he says, "[18] Some of you have become arrogant, as if I were not coming to you. [19] But I will come to you very soon, if the Lord is willing, and then I will find out not only how these arrogant people are talking, but <u>what power they have</u>. [20] For the kingdom of God is *not a matter of talk, but of power* [my emphasis]" (1 Corinthians

4:18-20). Paul is suggesting that God will back him up with the power of the Holy Spirit. It would not be a showdown of words, but something more supernatural or more spiritually powerful.[89]   I think quite a few "arguments" could be ended if God made it clearer whose side he was actually on or who was closer to the truth of the matter.[90] However, He loves his children equally and would prefer the dynamics

---

89 Paul told Elymas, the sorcerer, he would be blind for a season. This miracle of judgment was something Jesus did not do except to a fig tree. I am pretty sure that Paul's standing with God (complete surrender to suffering and his calling) carried spiritual weight. I think, in regard to Cessationism, the easiest/strongest point to be made is simply to invoke the Holy Spirit to convince the person. I have never done this, because it would confront the will of a person, and I am a big supporter of human free-will. To command the "spirit of division" to come out of a person would be an interesting experiment/experience, but I do not think it would be charitable to do so. Also, a person would not willingly receive the activity of the Holy Spirit if they are opposed to his activity. We are told not to "cast pearls", and it is ill advised to place a person in a situation which will bring judgment upon them if they reject the advances of the Holy Spirit.

90 "We see through a glass darkly." No one should arrogantly believe they have arrived at the correct definitive doctrine, especially in disputable matters.

of His relationship with us be a matter of our own choosing.

Ephesians 4 goes to talk about "not grieving the Holy Spirit." And this concept of grieving the Holy Spirit has to do with our language, it deals with anger and bitterness, which is expressed words. However, grieving the Holy Spirit can be done through brawling (quarreling),which carries the idea of clamorous argument. **Clamorous argument and slander, which is the word blasphemy in the Greek, is a form of speech that is accusatory and malicious and sometimes even aimed at God**. Instead, the scriptures state, "Be kind and compassionate to one another forgiving each other just as Christ forgave you." So it is necessary for heresy hunters to be "kind."

The word blasphemy has become commonly understood as being involved in speech or behavior that is injurious to the majesty of God. Jesus was accused of casting out demons by the Lord of the Flies (Satan). He tells the Pharisees that words against him will be forgiven, but blasphemy (slander) against the Holy Spirit would not be forgiven "in this age and the age to come."[91] So it is one thing to slander the

---

91 Matthew the 12:31 says that "blasphemy against the Holy Spirit will not be forgiven in this age or the age to

235

vessel or instrument of God, it is another to slander the source behind the vessel. In essence, if you are going to slander (and you shouldn't), it is better to slander a person (Charismatic) than it is to suggest that the Holy Spirit is actually a "spirit of error" or a demon.

Moving on from the subject of slander and accusation, Paul suggests that brawling (quarreling) or clamorous argument is part of the old self and should not be practiced. In a pastoral word to his spiritual son Titus, Paul tells him, "[9] But *avoid foolish controversies* and genealogies and *arguments* and quarrels about the law, because these are unprofitable and useless. [10] **Warn a divisive person**

---

come". You can speak against the Son of Man Jesus told the Pharisees, but if you speak a word of blasphemy against the Holy Spirit you will not be forgiven in this age and the age to come. The context is the Pharisees were were assigning the work of the Holy Spirit to the Devil. Literally, a man was freed from demons, the power and glory of God came upon him and they looked at the glory of God and, evidently without reservation of their heart, they publicly said the devil was the cause or root of the activity that freed the man. The glory/work of God that brought freedom, life, wholeness, joy, and restoration to this man, is said to be the work of Satan and not the Holy Spirit. It is blasphemy to say the Holy Spirit is Satan; it is saying the Spirit of Truth is the Father of Lies.

once, and then warn them a second time. After that, *have nothing to do with them.* ¹¹ You may be sure that **such people are warped and sinful**; they are self-condemned [my emphasis]" (Titus 3:9-11 NIV). Paul is giving counsel to one who has been entrusted with the pastoral care of people, who are under his authority. A divisive person, in a time when the church was closely connected and represented the body of Christ in that city, could easily ruin a fellowship. Paul tells Titus to warn the divisive person once and after the second warning he tells Titus not to associate with that person. Associating with a divisive person will cause one to "catch" that same spirit of dissension.⁹² Destroying the unity of God's people is a serious matter. Paul said a lack of recognition of the body resulted in death when taking the Lord's Supper in an inappropriate manner (1 Cor. 11:17-34). Ananias and Saphira both lost their lives for lying to the Holy Spirit in trying to gain status in the fellowship (Acts 5:1-5).

---

92 While the higher critical thinking skills involved in debate are commendable, I have to wonder about the spirit of debate when it encourages winning an argument at all costs in order to be the best in the competition. I don't believe that debate, in and of itself, is bad, but if an individual tends to be prideful or arrogant, debate will bring out the most obnoxious qualities of that individual.

Additionally, some of the tactics that are used in making an argument are not truthful. It has been said that a half-truth is as good as a lie. Taking someone's words out of context, spinning an accusation around a "strawman" position, and deceptive misrepresentation are all a form of lying, Satan is the "Father [source] of Lies." Paul states, "Therefore each of you must put off falsehood and speak truthfully to your neighbor, for we are all members of one body" (Eph. 4:25). The word for falsehood is falsity—**pseudo** in the Greek language. It is words that are partially true, true words set in a false contexts, or a half truth, where a part is missing which changes the nature of what is spoken. It can be that which is left unspoken, which causes the true words that are spoken to be false. So lying is more prevalent than we realize. We are to continuously reject, in the Greek it is translated, reject or put off continuously, falsity (falsehood). It is almost impossible to correctly discern the motives of others, which makes misrepresentation highly probable in the criticism of any ministry. That is why Paul counsels believers not to criticize other people/ministries, when he states, "⁴ Who are you to judge someone else's servant? To their own master, servants stand or fall. And they will stand, for the Lord is able to make them stand" (Romans 14:4). The principle here is

Paul is maintaining that the Lord Jesus Christ is the only true and righteous judge. Instead of judging people or ministries pray that our common master will take care of his own servants.[93]

Furthermore, even if Charismatics are your enemy, you should love and bless them, not curse them. To curse someone is <u>to imprecate evil upon, to announce doom, to speak evil consequences upon another or another's activities</u>. This is the word that is used in James 3:10 about blessing and cursing; We are <u>forbidden</u> **to curse others**. We are, instead, to bless those that speak evil and imprecate doom upon us. Jesus said bless them. For the sake of unity, maybe the opposing camps need to make large financial contributions to each others ministries (what a bazaar and uncomfortable idea). Hmmmm. . . do good to those who are your enemies. Jesus says

---

93 The context if Romans 14 has to do with disputable matters (meat offered to idols). It gives believers the uncomfortable option of obeying their conscience and not the conscience of others while at the same time not being offensive to each other. So, let the Charismatics practice their disputable tongues in faith and do not judge them, while they are not to judge evangelicals for not speaking in tongues because it is a disputable matter. Whatever is not done in faith is sin. If you don't have the faith for it, then don't do it; don't violate your conscience.

in Luke 6:35-36, "³⁵ But love your enemies, *do good to them* [my emphasis], and lend to them without expecting to get anything back [sounds like making a contribution to me]. Then your reward will be great, and you will be children of the Most High, because he is kind to the ungrateful and wicked. ³⁶ Be merciful, just as your Father is merciful." Maybe a dialogue could begin to take place and the excesses of the Charismatic movement could be dealt with and the richness of the Charismatic experience could be enjoyed by Evangelicals.

Perhaps, as an evangelical, you are not in the Cessationist camp, but simply want to keep Jesus and the cross the focus of your belief system. For you, evangelism and the Great Commission is the priority. You have checked your heart and you know that you are not motivated by fear of experiencing something new in regard to the Holy Spirit. Neither are you harboring any anger for an offense you gained from a "Spirit-oriented" person or church. You know that you are not judgmental or arrogant in your doctrine. You just want to see people won to Jesus, and these other things are a distraction, in your opinion. I think it is important to re-envision the Great Commission, if that is the case.

First of all, the main operative participle in the great commission is not evangelism, but the making of disciples. Discipleship begins with salvation, followed by baptism, and continues through the process of being taught how to live one's life consistently with the commands of Jesus. The commission is to make disciples not just get people saved. So, the question is: How are you making disciples when you consider Matthew 28:18-20? This passage states "[18] Then Jesus came to them and said, 'All authority in heaven and on earth has been given to me.[19] Therefore go and make disciples of all nations, baptizing them in the name of the Father and of the Son and of the Holy Spirit, [20] and teaching them to obey everything I have commanded you. And surely I am with you always, to the very end of the age.'" If you will notice the great commission begins with Jesus asserting his authority (exercised authority is backed up with his power-Luke 9:1-2). The force of the Greek assumes that believers will be going and should be translated thusly, "as you go [assumption] make disciples [command]." How do you make disciples? Jesus tells us, "[teach] them to obey everything I have commanded you." We are to teach new converts to do everything that Jesus told the disciples to do, that is, obey his every command that was delivered to his disciples. What did He command the disciples to do? When Jesus had called the Twelve together, he gave them power and authority to drive out all demons and to cure diseases, ² and he sent them out to proclaim the kingdom of God and to heal the sick (Luke 9:1-2). Perhaps you noticed that there are no commands in this passage only an enablement for the disciples to do the ministry. Okay. Let's look at where Jesus gives his disciples a similar charge in the form of a command. "⁵ These twelve Jesus sent out with the following instructions: "Do not go among the Gentiles or enter any town of the Samaritans. ⁶ Go rather to the lost sheep of Israel. ⁷ As you go, proclaim this message: 'The kingdom of heaven has come near.' ⁸ Heal the sick, raise the dead, cleanse those who have leprosy, drive out demons. Freely you have received; freely give" (Matthew 10:5-8). Clearly, the structure of this charge is to proclaim, heal, raise, cleanse, and drive out. All of these terms are in a imperative or command tense in the Greek. Perhaps, you would like to qualify this passage as referring only to the "lost sheep of Israel."[94] However, being the witnesses of Jesus extended from Jerusalem, Judea,

---

94 Matthew's gospel is written specifically from a Jewish perspective because he wants to reach the Jews. No such qualifier is mentioned in the gospel of Luke because he was writing to a more gentile audience. Furthermore, it is clear that the ministry of Paul, and Peter for that matter, extended the commands of Jesus to include a gentile population.

242

Samaria to the uttermost parts of the earth (Acts 1:8—8 "But you will receive power when the Holy Spirit comes on you; and you will be my witnesses in Jerusalem, and in all Judea and Samaria, and to the ends of the earth"). Additionally, the closing promise of the Great commission states, "And surely I am with you always, to the very end of the age (NIV) or "and, lo, I am with you always, even unto the end of the world" (KJV).

The unpleasant news, for evangelicals, is that if the evangelical church is not training believers in casting out demons, healing the sick, or proclaiming the gospel of the kingdom (we run into few lepers and dead people on a regular basis), then the church is disobedient to the commands of Christ and are inadequately making disciples after the pattern of Jesus. However, it is not possible to do the supernatural ministry of Jesus apart from the power of the Holy Spirit ("you shall be clothed with power from on high" (Luke 24:49) and "You shall receive power when the Holy Spirit is come upon you to be my witnesses" (Acts 1:8). How can Evangelicals tap into the power of the Holy Spirit, who already lives inside of them? This question will be explored in the next chapter.

243

Chapter 11: Being Filled with the Holy Spirit Evangelical Style

Paul says in Ephesians 5:17-18a, "¹⁷ Therefore do not be foolish, but understand what the Lord's will is. ¹⁸ Do not get drunk on wine, which leads to debauchery. Instead, be filled with the Spirit." The Greek grammar of "be filled" is a present continuous imperative, meaning you are commanded to be constantly or repeatedly filled with the Holy Spirit. Okay, as an evangelical, how can you painlessly walk in the power of the Holy Spirit and keep your favorite reformed doctrine? Well, first of all, if you are uncomfortable with speaking in tongues, you very likely won't; I didn't speak in tongues when I was filled/empowered by the Spirit. Instead of speaking in tongues, I began to see people healed when I prayed for them. So, let's take on the next reformed issue with the filling of the Holy Spirit—the term "Baptism with the Holy Spirit." Now, from my experience, my "filling" was a definite experience of empowerment. It happened suddenly, and it appears to me to be a subsequent experience to my conversion experience.

244

However, if you only want to maintain one initial baptism with the Holy Spirit (indwelling that occurs at salvation), it is primarily a matter of terminology or semantics. Evangelical scholars acknowledge that there are many "fillings" of the Holy Spirit after the first filling. So, if you liked your conversion "filling" of the Holy Spirit, how about another one; the second one is a doozey. You don't even have to call it another coming of the Holy Spirit or a second/subsequent experience with the Holy Spirit (even though chronologically if one filling occurs after the other it will be subsequent). Perhaps you will want to say that you simply yielded to a greater level of influence of the Holy Spirit already in you. If, however, as was true in my case, you find that simply claiming that you are filled with the Holy Spirit does not result in your ability to perform supernatural tasks, then perhaps you should consider a more passionate pursuit in your relationship with the Holy Spirit, keeping in mind that there are subsequent infillings of the Holy Spirit, whatever you want to call them. Why not ask the Holy Spirit to fill you, since you can have more than one filling?

In fact, according to the Scriptures, there is more than one baptism. Now, evangelicals claim there is a water baptism and a baptism that places you into the body of Christ or the conversion experience.

245

Being Filled with the Holy Spirit Evangelical Style

There is nothing in Scripture to suggest that there are only two kinds of baptism, however. In Hebrews 6:1-2 it states, "Therefore leaving the principles of the doctrine of Christ, let us go on unto perfection; not laying again the foundation of repentance from dead works, and of faith toward God,² Of the doctrine of *baptisms*,[plural; my emphasis] and of laying on of hands, and of resurrection of the dead, and of eternal judgment" (KJV). In Matthew 3:11 it states, ¹¹ I indeed baptize you with water unto repentance, but he that cometh after me is mightier than I, whose shoes I am not worthy to bear: he shall baptize you with the Holy Ghost, and with fire" (KJV). Here we see the possibility of three baptisms: one of water, one of the Holy Spirit, and one of fire. In this instance, I have chosen the King James Version (a more popular version among the very conservative) because of the grammatical structure of the sentence (in this case, the Holy Spirit and fire are separated). Other translations simply say that Jesus will baptize with the Holy Spirit and fire. It is possible that the Holy Spirit and fire are combined as one expression and comprise one experience. However, it is also possible that they are two separate experiences. Fire is a symbol of the Holy Spirit. According to Acts 2:3 "³ And divided tongues as of *fire appeared to them and rested on each one of them.* ⁴ And they were all *filled with the Holy Spirit* [my emphasis] and began to speak in other tongues as the Spirit gave them utterance. This is commonly seen among evangelicals as the indwelling of the Holy Spirit or the birth of the church. At this point, if we are to understand that indwelling represents conversion, the disciples, inclusive of 120 people, became Christians at the coming of the Holy Spirit at Pentecost. This doesn't really seem to make sense theologically or in terms of the terminology that Luke uses in his gospel and the book of Acts. Luke 24:49 records Jesus as saying, "⁴⁹ I am going to send you what my Father has promised; but stay in the city until you have been *clothed with power* [my emphasis] from on high." Jesus does not say "indwelt by the Holy Spirit from on high." Later, Luke writes in Acts 1:8 "⁸ But *you will receive power* when the Holy Spirit has *come upon you*, [my emphasis] and you will be my witnesses in Jerusalem and in all Judea and Samaria, and to the end of the earth." Notice, once again, the emphasis is on power and not indwelling. In both passages, the terms "clothed" and "upon you" do not seem to convey an indwelling experience. In fact, when we return to Acts 2:3 "³ And divided tongues as of *fire appeared to them and* <u>rested on</u> *each one of them.* ⁴ And they were all *filled with the Holy Spirit,*" we read that the spirit rested ON them, and this experience is called

247

being "filled with the Holy Spirit." At this point, the question that comes to mind is: if this experience is not an indwelling, when did it occur? In John 20:21-22, it states, "²¹ Jesus said to them again, 'Peace be with you. As the Father has sent me, even so I am sending you.' ²² And when he had said this, he breathed on them and said to them, 'Receive the Holy Spirit.'" Here, we see that Jesus commands his disciples to receive the Holy Spirit. In the Greek, the word *lambano* is in the ingressive tense conveying the imperative mood or command. The ingressive tense has to do with an initializing action, a foretaste or beginning experience. Jesus does not say they are to receive "power from on high" in this instance. He tells them to receive the Holy Spirit. The word for breath in the Greek is connected with the word *pneuma*, which may be translated spirit or wind. I believe that God backed up Jesus' command to receive the Holy Spirit, and I believe that by blowing on them something actually took place. Jesus was not using a metaphor or a prophetic action of what was going to take place in the future at Pentecost, even though some might claim this was the case. If the two experiences are separated, one is "baptized with the Holy Spirit" and the other "baptized with fire" (Matthew 3:11), then there is a subsequent work of the Holy Spirit, as John 20:21-22 suggests followed by Acts 2:3-4.[95] If you combined the two as simply the indwelling of the Holy Spirit, in my experience, you will either get a powerless Evangelicalism or radical Pentecostalism claiming that evangelicals are not saved because they are not filled with the Spirit with evidence of speaking in tongues. For me, both these positions are undesirable, if not untenable. Is there a solution?

It seems that the biggest objection to the

---

95 A study of the Feasts of Israel, applying them to the progression of the Christian life, shows a separation between the Feast of Passover and the Feast of Pentecost. The Feast of Passover had three components: the eating of the Passover meal (death of the lamb), the removal of leaven from the house (forgiveness of sin), and first fruits, which is tied to the resurrection. This feast is tied to conversion and the indwelling of the Holy Spirit. The Feast of Pentecost occurred at Mt. Sinai where God showed up in power as fire descended on the mountain. Kevin Conner in his book *The Feasts of Israel* has an in-depth discussion on this matter and its application to the Christian life. The 40 days of Jesus teaching his disciples, post crucifixion, followed by the ten days of waiting for the coming of the Holy Spirit is 50 days (hence, the word penta in Pentecost). It is also the time represented by Israel's journey to Mt Sinai after being delivered from Egypt (the Passover). In Jewish history, the two events and feasts are separate.

subsequent work of the Spirit, beyond conversion, is the mistaken notion that somehow you get more of the Spirit than what you already have. This notion is based on the idea that somehow the Holy Spirit is a quantity (as in being a quart low and in need of being filled or topped off) and not a person. Furthermore, the Holy Spirit is not only IN a person, he is AROUND the person. If the Holy Spirit on the outside wants to link up with the Holy Spirit on the inside, and chooses to ignore material/physical boundaries, then you don't receive more of the "substance" of the Holy Spirit, who is already in you, but instead you receive a greater awareness of the intensity of the Holy Spirit both in you and spilling out into the natural realm (thus, supernatural experiences and ministry). A simple shift in paradigm allows you to "have your cake and eat it too." In Ephesians 1: 3, Paul states, "³ Blessed be the God and Father of our Lord Jesus Christ, who has blessed us in Christ with every spiritual blessing in the heavenly places." In this passage, the structure of the grammar suggests that we already have every spiritual blessing. If that is the case, why are some people's experiences different than other people's experiences? The answer is simple: you have to appropriate that which already belongs to you. For example, we have been completely forgiven of all our sin, yet we have to confess our sins in order to receive (appropriate) the promise of being forgiven and cleansed (1 John 1:9). By faith, we access the promises of God and everything that Jesus Christ paid for by his death on the cross. Salvation exists; however, people must appropriate the salvation that already exists for them by faith. If there is a continuing work of grace, such as sanctification, which exists apart from our own human effort, there must be a level of cooperation to allow the Holy Spirit to do that work in us. The work of the Holy Spirit can be enhanced through the exercise of the spiritual disciplines such as prayer, worship, fasting, meditation and the study of the Scriptures, but these practices cannot be considered the grace provided by the Holy Spirit that brings about transformation. We live a life, by faith, which allows us to appropriate that grace of God. I use the term grace not just in terms of unmerited favor, but also in terms of divine enablement. If God gives us divine enablement, it is not a nebulous concept that comes from him, but this grace is actually the Holy Spirit. So in a sense, we appropriate or receive from God increases of his manifest presence, or grace, which enables us to grow into the image of Jesus Christ. Once we repackage the concepts that allow us to better understand how the Holy Spirit can work in manifold and diverse ways, then we can stop arguing

251

Being Filled with the Holy Spirit Evangelical Style

about the precious life of the Holy Spirit (this treasure in clay vessels) and get on with the more important task of being sure that we are constantly filled with the Holy Spirit. While my empowerment came suddenly, my spiritual son Cody Persell was filled by a gradual process, which is more in keeping with a reformed theological perspective. The testimony of his spiritual pursuit of being filled with the Spirit, over time, is the subject of the next chapter.

Epilogue: Pursuing the Fullness of Christ: By Cody Persell

Throughout the years, God has honored and blessed my pursuit of Him. He has and continues to be gracious to me as I seek to know Him and His ways. As much as I have tried to, in my pursuit of Him, God is not One that we can put into a theological box; He doesn't fit! He desires to be pursued and discovered. The mysteries of God and the uniqueness of each Christian—personality and experiences—doesn't allow us to take a masterpiece artwork full of vibrant colors and life and dull it down to a black and white replica calling it "The Doctrines of God." As much as we want our understanding of God to be black and white or cut and dry, He is beyond that. This is the beauty of pursuing God.

I remember having a conversation with my wife early in our relationship before we were married about the existence of the supernatural spiritual gifts in the church today. While my wife leaned more toward the continuationist side and me the cessationist, we both agreed that there was something missing in

253

the church. With our denominational background both in church attendance and college education, much was skipped concerning this conversation, and the authors we read and trusted did not address this issue with much detail, leaving us wanting and uncertain at best.

My early Christian journey consisted of searching out the knowledge of God. I had a strong desire to know the Scriptures and to know God. We found some pastors and leaders who were open but cautious to the spiritual gifts, but we would steer clear from any charismatic authors because supposedly their doctrine was weak and hype-focused. It wasn't until a few years later that we discovered that there are pastors and leaders who were both concerned with sound doctrine and were experiencing charismatic phenomena and implementing spiritual gifts in their churches. I discovered that sound doctrine *included* charismatic experiences and spiritual gifts. In fact, I learned that I was interpreting scripture from my experiences (in this case the lack thereof) the very thing that I was taught not to do in my Bible classes. As a young, arm-chair theologian, who thought he had all his theological ducks in a row, I found myself starting over. I had to approach the Scriptures with a fresh start.

I met Dr. Thomas Reedy in 2005 where he

and I taught high school English together. As a result, we spent much time together developing curriculum and completing projects for the English department. There were rumors that Dr. Reedy was a *charis-maniac* – he believed in the Holy Spirit and the charismatic gifts. Interestingly enough, while I didn't believe in charismatic phenomena, I did believe in demonic oppression, and he would come to the morning devotional describing experiences he had the night before in casting demons out of individuals. Because of my own encounters with demonic spirits, I knew that they were real and their influences were real. This led to numerous conversations about exorcisms or what he described as deliverance ministry, and he had a Biblical explanation for the spiritual gifts still existing today. This launched me on a journey of studying the scriptures, reading books on spiritual gifts and eventually my wife and I receiving training by Tom in inner healing/deliverance ministry. Additionally, and more importantly, this launched me on a journey of finding my identity in Christ and looking deeply at my inward life and dealing with wounds and demonic spirits that were hindering areas of my own life.

I still remember today the first deliverance session that Amy (my wife) and I observed after receiving training in inner healing and deliverance.

Epilogue

The only grid that we had for deliverance was what was portrayed in the cinema. Amy and I were both nervous as we discovered that the client was hindered in reading the word. Every time she would try to read the Scriptures, she would get extremely sleepy and/or painful headaches. As they began to pray for her, I was curious about what was going to take place. After an extended time-frame of expulsive behavior, she was set free. After seeing her set free from a demonic influence and able to read the word, I was even more convinced about supernatural phenomena and the need for spirituals gifts. From this point, I wanted to learn everything that I could about spiritual warfare and continued to pursue deliverance ministry. We continued in ministry with Tom and assisted him with numerous ministry sessions and discovered spiritual giftings that the Lord had given us, namely the gift of prophesy (words of knowledge) and discernment of spirits. The Lord began to more consistently reveal wounds and demonic hindrances before we would have a conversation with the one receiving ministry through prophetic visions and prophetic impressions and sensing demonic spirits.

Since 2006, Tom Reedy has mentored me in supernatural ministry and the Lord has used him to help me discover a calling that God has on my life, namely being used of the Lord in helping others walk in their identity in Christ. It has been an incredible journey of discovering the truth of scriptures and experiencing God in tangible ways. Tom and I have been able to minister to numerous individuals as well as train others in supernatural ministry especially the ministry of inner healing and deliverance. It is our desire to see others walk in the fullness of God—to live the abundant life that Christ purchased on the cross, and I am thankful that the Lord has allowed our paths to cross.

Afterward

I began writing this book in 2004 and stopped after a few chapters (I began to have other writing projects on my mind), but Cody encouraged me to finish this book because, in his estimation, it was very much needed. Cody still has friends of a Baptist persuasion, while many of my connections along these lines were decades old. In my early days, I am sure I was zealous to extol my experiences in the supernatural life and ministry of the Holy Spirit because of how wonderful it was. Some took offense because, apparently, they felt like something was being said about their relationship with Christ that I did not intend. As I am much older now, I find no need to be a crusader to promote the reality of living a life in the supernatural realm of the Holy Spirit. I could call it discernment; I could call it being disinterested in trying to help someone go some place he or she is unwilling to go. Jesus did not pour his life into trying to convince his critics; He devoted his life to the spiritually hungry. Undoubtedly, this book will make some people angry, and it will make some people hungry and open to pursue the Holy Spirit. These are free-will choices that people make. I do not assume responsibility for those choices. Whether angry or hopeful, study the scriptures for yourself and do it in humility, prayer and openness to what God wants to show you. Originally, (in 2004) my desire was to help evangelicals who were open to the Holy Spirit to answer the question: Why is it that it seems I can only go so far in regard to the ministry of the Holy Spirit? However, over the last ten years, I have noticed, because of the increase in the amount of deliverance ministry among Christians, that there seems to be an active spiritual opposition from the enemy in regard to the things of the Holy Spirit. It is possible that some of the additional chapters may be more provocative.

Additionally, my teaching responsibilities for the last four years have been in the field of apologetics. By nature, apologetics (a defense of the faith) is based in argument. Furthermore, my graduate work is in the field of rhetoric (argument and logic, with a tinge of philosophy). I hope my tone has been reasonable, but I admit to some degree I am a provocateur. My job is to get students to think, and the only way to do that is to challenge their thinking processes. In terms of my students, whatever their belief system is (as long as it is fundamentally orthodox), it matters to me that their own belief system belong to them and not just a belief in consensus theology.[96] I teach at an institution that values diversity within orthodoxy; in that sense our faculty has a broad denominational background. In the student body, while I have never found evangelical unbelief objectionable, I sometimes find there are those who find my Charismatic beliefs objectionable.[97] No one

---

96 Consensus theology is where someone believes something not based on thorough examination of scripture, but simple because they were exposed to a culture or influence of respected persons within a certain group to which they belong. Acceptance of a system of belief without rigorous examination will be weak in the face of competing ideologies that students face in the college environment. Too many Christian students are abandoning their faith when they leave home and go off to college. My goal is to expose them to a myriad of positions and provide an opportunity to apply the scriptures and the methods available to evaluate truth claims.

97 I personally object to unbelief, nominal Christianity, fuzzy thinking, and smug, pharisaical evangelical attitudes that I sometimes run across. I have seen some evangelicals smirk at the worship style of Charismatics—I mean really? I do not report these individuals to the administration or confront them. The problem is evangelicalism is the lowest common denominator upon which we all can

is a walking argument against anyone else. We are all members of the body of Christ. If there is agitation it does not come from the Lord; I suggest one should look elsewhere. "Great peace have they which love thy law: and nothing shall offend them" (Psalms 119:165 KJV).

Jack Deere in his book *Surprised by the Power of the Holy Spirit* suggests that the main reason for unbelief or Cessationism is simple: a lack of experience (57). After years teaching at Dallas Theological Seminary (a Cessationist school), Deere not only experienced the power of the Holy Spirit, but when he asked students why they held their particular theological views, they were not able to give a reason from scripture for their beliefs. They simply held to a consensus theology. Perhaps it is time to develop a hunger for all three persons of the Trinity, and spend some time examining the scripture under the Holy Spirit's guidance (1 John 2:20--But you have an anointing from the Holy One, and all of you know the truth). As an evangelical why is this book important to you? Aside from personal

---

agree. Therefore evangelicals are supported 100% for their theological beliefs, while Charismatic/Pentecostals must adhere to a kind of censorship on some of their orthodox beliefs in institutions that are interested in a "unity" perspective within a non-denominational context.

261

benefits, the church is facing challenges today in an unprecedented way.

The millennial generation will pose a particular challenge to churches that emphasize doctrine and traditional ways of doing ministry and services. Studies show that the Millennials privilege experience over doctrine. This is reinforced by the tendency to connect with stories (narratives or parables) over a more structured logo-centric sermon. Because the highest value in this generation is toleration, epistemological certainty (the attitude that you know you are right while others are wrong about a matter) tends to cause Millennials to shy away from doctrine and ethical/moral preaching that is seen as intolerant of others. They are somewhat jaded in regard to trusting authority and do not respond well to being told "because the bible says . . .", which they view as having many interpretations and as having been used by preachers to promote their own agenda. Consequently, Millennials do not have a sense of loyalty to any one church or denomination. They are willing to attend the churches of their friends even though the church might be a different denomination or have a different doctrine. Part of the problem is that the Millennial generation has been given the impression that they are special to the point of creating a kind of narcissism. They are the digital generation; they know how to use technology more than the adults in their lives. They can quickly access information through the internet and do not need to rely on teachers or traditional modes of education. Millennials value their friendships and relationships among their peers more than they value programs. They are interested in their own agenda and getting out of religion what is beneficial to them, which means rich meaningful connections with people in a loving or at least accepting environment. They are not content to simply sit in church and have someone speak at them. Compounding this problem for the traditional church is the development of a limited attention span. Millennials have been inundated with glitzy highly polished content on the internet. They are more pop cultural in their approach to life than having a well thought out worldview. Because church seems like it is "selling them a vision or a program," and not relational, they have become disinterested in church attendance. They are more likely to attend non-traditional gatherings in people's homes (house churches) where they can participate, share life, tell stories, and have dialogue about the faith without having an authority or structure.

Everything I have stated so far is based on studies that look at the general characteristics of the Millennial generation. There are exceptions to what I have stated among many Millennials. However, as you can see by the portrait that has been painted of this generation, the traditional church is faced with a daunting task. To complicate matters, what Millennials want or are comfortable with has unintended consequences which causes them at times to pull in the opposite direction. They want relationships but the 500+ friends they have on Facebook is both a lure and a lack of true friendship. Technology in terms of the cell phone means they keep in touch more often, but using the texting function means they do not hear each other's voices. I have seen groups of adolescents sitting in a restaurant or standing together at a Starbucks using their cell phones (checking Facebook, texting, looking at youtube etc.) and not holding any kind of conversation with their friends. The emphasis on toleration has caused them, at times, to be morally adrift. They are drenched in pluralism and a plethora of divergent opinions to the point that there does not seem to be only one correct answer. This undermines the sense of purpose and a guiding compass for their lives. They are looking for something authentic but have a problem with absolutes.[98] They want to be

98 Relativism (the idea there are no absolute standards that apply to everyone at all times) has been around

able to give their lives to some important cause, but environmentalism, human equality, and world peace are too humanistic to actually satisfy deeper spiritual longing.[99] What can be done to address these issues and reach the Millennial generation?

Many different strategies have been tried. To appeal to the technological savvy Millennials, who are into pop culture, some churches have become "seeker sensitive" creating services that "pop" so as not to bore Millennials. Services become a smorgasbord (variety) of presentations. This appeals also to the narcissistic tendency of Millennials, but does not challenge them to give

---

since the 1960s with Fletcher's "situation ethics" and "values based" education in public schools. It means all morals and principles for living one's life is specific only to the needs and desires of the individual or his or her value system. Something may be wrong for one person and perfectly okay for someone else. This kind of moral anarchy is what informs toleration.

99 Conservative evangelicals were shocked to find out that environmentalism was more important to younger evangelicals than the issues of abortion and gay rights. Consequently, young adult evangelical voters are more independent in their voting practices and will not use abortion as a litmus test for choosing who they will vote for.

their lives over to something higher than themselves. Non-denominational churches, especially the mega-churches, sometimes appeal to the Millennials. Such churches usually have a more diverse ethnic population, more opportunities to do non-traditional ministry (television, radio, sports, drama, bands etc), and have a larger budget to accommodate the needs and desires of Millennials.[100] However, there is some bad news.

A recent report asserts that this generation, like previous generations of young people, abandons their faith during the college years. However, unlike previous generations, they are not coming back to the church after they get married and have children. Statistically, a fewer number of those who stop going to church are returning to the church. Additionally, the "Emergent Church" is attracting Millennials because it fits into their value system. Emergent church leaders like Brian Maclearen and Rob Bell have constructed a church movement that is governed by Millennial concerns. Rob Bell has suggested there

---

100 Smaller congregations tend to be ethnically homogeneous. The good news is some of the mega churches, although they do not have a denominational tag, are clearly evangelical. The evangelical message is broad enough to take in many different "kinds" of Christians, making the church somewhat inter-denominational.

might not be a hell and has promoted a tolerant kind of universalism that suggests there may be more than one way to get to "heaven." This is not, however, the main concern of the Emergent church anyway. They are more interested in harmonious relationships here and now than they are in eternity. This "hipster" brand of Christianity is pushing all the right buttons for Millennials. Not only are they tolerant, they have epistemological humility, i.e., they are willing to leave open the possibility that it is okay not to know for sure if one's doctrines are absolutely true. They emphasize dialogue. They want to talk with you and not at you. Doctrine is too sterile for them; they want to convey truth in the form of stories about life, and everyone's story is valid. Church life is about relationships and being together and a kind of self actualization. The Christian faith is not about certainty, but about the journey. Using the bible as an authority "to beat up on" or prove that you are right is distasteful to this movement. I am sure there is much more to the Emergent Church than what I have addressed here. And there are some excellent books on this movement and you can read their own materials and decide for yourself. This church movement, however, is seeking to draw Millennials into their fold. The question is: How can the evangelical church be faithful to the gospel and the scriptures and still reach this Millennial generation? The answer is authentic relationships that reflect applied scripture connected to their experience, and an emphasis the promotes an experiential and vibrate encounter with the living God/Christ by way of the Holy Spirit.

Even more problematic is a systemic weakness in the church as a whole. While I served as a Baptist pastor and was involved in graduate work at the seminary I learned two things about the denomination that were disconcerting. The first thing I learned was that about 50% of the members had not attended church in over a year (you can be an inactive member in this denomination, i.e., be counted as a member whether or not you ever participate). This particular denomination, at the time, prided itself in being the largest evangelical denomination in the country. However, statistically, how can one make that claim when you do not know the status of 50% of your members? The second matter that was disconcerting was that church growth specialists claimed that a large majority of the growth of congregations was due to either "biological growth" (the offspring of parents populating the church programs) or "transfer growth" (members from other churches transferring their membership into the church). In short, there was a lack of "conversion growth" in the denomination that was unabashedly evangelistic in its approach to Christian ministry. I still remember asking my congregation of 95 people to raise their hands if they led anyone to Christ in the past year. One or two people raised their hands. I trained a different congregation in the Baptist version of Evangelism Explosion (created by Presbyterian pastor D. James Kennedy) and in the methods of Campus Crusade. The class was well attended, but when it came time to go and share our faith, no one showed up. Stories like this do not prove anything, but, instead, invites the reader to ask some questions about his or her own congregation. If a significant number of people are being saved in your congregation that is great. Let me ask you a question, however. Are these people being saved as a part of the services or is the membership involved in evangelism?[101] If the pastor has an evangelist gifting, then most of the sermons will have a gospel presentation even if the sermon is on tithing. He will be supernaturally gifted and motivated to reach people and that usually transfers to the congregation.

---

101 Sometimes parishioners believe it is the job of the pastor to evangelize or their responsibility is simply to invite the lost to church to hear the gospel (the preaching ministry of the pastor). Jesus did not say come and hear; he told his disciples to go and tell.

Afterward

But the evangelist is not a teacher. New converts must be discipled. The tragedy is that some new converts fall away because they are not discipled adequately. I remember an evangelism-oriented church and pastor that lead the city in conversions and baptisms in the hundreds, but their membership statistics only showed a marginal increase. Additionally, the pastor who is an evangelist will tend to preach the basic tenets of the gospel but the members of the congregation need to only be "saved" once. This causes them to seek out other congregations that will help them grow spiritually (transfer growth), much to the chagrin of some evangelical churches, their members might even consider Charismatic churches to meet their spiritual needs. Okay, so what is my point? The evangelical church needs to change and I suggest that change needs to be a true Holy Spirit revival that leads to a reformation of evangelical culture.

I am not talking about some of the most common Charismatic churches as being at the forefront of this change. I recently attended a "Pentecostal-type" denomination and found it to be more evangelical than anything else. Their doctrine affirms the Baptism of the Holy Spirit and even healing, but not much of either is occurring on a regular basis. Their message of love and service to

270

the community could easily fit into any evangelical agenda. Here is the point. They are growing and making an impact on the community. The pastor and the congregation seek God's direction and trust in the life of the Holy Spirit, but operate in a way that would please most evangelicals. Thus, I am saying that evangelical ministry values can still be consistent with the leadership and supernatural ministry of the Holy Spirit. More and more evangelical churches are incorporating Charismatic-type worship in their services and are even removing the denominational tag off their signs (they stay in the denomination, but do not want to attract traditional denominationalists or dissuade those who do not want to be labeled). Furthermore, I do not agree with some of the strange twists in theology or practices represented by some Charismatic-type churches. In essence, seek God and his Spirit; do not blindly conform to a theological pattern (consensus) of someone else.

Works Cited/Suggested Reading

Brand, Chad Owen. Ed. *Perspectives on Spirit Baptism: Five Views.* Nashville: Broadman and Holman P, 2004.

DeArteaga, William. *Quenching the Spirit: Discover the REAL Spirit behind the Charismatic Controversy*. Orlando: Creation House, 1992.

Deere, Jack. *Surprised by the Power of the Holy Spirit: Discovering How God Speaks and Heals Today.* Grand Rapids: Zondervan P., 1993.

Kraft, Charles H. *Christianity with Power:Your Worldview and Your Experience of the Supernatural*. Ann Arbor, MI: Vine Books/ Servant Publications, 1989.

Pearcey, Nancy. *Total Truth: Liberating Christianity from Its Cultural Captivity*. Wheaton: Crossway Books/Good News P, 2004.

Robinson, Ras. *How to Receive God's Anointing*. Fort Worth: Fullness House. 1985

Wagner, C. Peter. *The Third Wave of the Holy Spirit: Discovering the Power of Signs and Wonders*. Ann Arbor, MI: Servant P. 1988

Wimber, John. *Power Evangelism*. Ventura, CA: Regal/Gospel Light P, 2009.

More Books by Thomas Reedy

COMING SOON...

- Healing and Freedom for the Wounded Heart

- The Five Fold Ministry and the Armor of God

- The Apostle: Metaphors of an Emergent Ministry

For more additional information on requesting ministry for your church, contact us at

roarpublications@gmail.com

Made in the USA
Charleston, SC
13 March 2015